INDIAN ART
of the United States

INDIAN ART
of the United States

BY FREDERIC H. DOUGLAS
AND RENE D'HARNONCOURT

THE MUSEUM OF MODERN ART · NEW YORK

THE TITLE PAGE ILLUSTRATION IS A NORTH-
WEST-COAST CARVED WOODEN MASK LENT BY
THE MILWAUKEE PUBLIC MUSEUM

AUTHORS' NOTE: The authors of this book have attempted
to give a representative picture of Indian art in the United
States. Since some of the tribal groups live both in the
United States and in Canada, a number of significant Canadian specimens have been included in order to show the
entire scope of each culture. One ancient Eskimo ivory object was actually collected in Siberia, but was undoubtedly
made by an Alaskan Eskimo.   F. H. D.   R. D' H.

Contents

Acknowledgments

The exhibition upon which this book is based has been prepared by the Indian Arts and Crafts Board of the United States Department of the Interior, under the direction of the General Manager, Mr. René d'Harnoncourt, in collaboration with Mr. Frederic H. Douglas, Curator of Indian Art of the Denver Art Museum, and Mr. Henry Klumb, Architect.

Commissioners of the Indian Arts and Crafts Board of the United States Department of the Interior: Hon. John Collier, *Chairman;* Hon. Ebert K. Burlew, Dr. A. V. Kidder, Mr. James W. Young, Mr. Lorenzo Hubbell.

Sponsoring Institutions: The United States National Museum, Washington, D. C.; The Royal Ontario Museum of Archaeology, Toronto.

Lenders and Cooperating Institutions: Mr. William H. Clafin, Jr., Belmont, Massachusetts; Mrs. William Denman, San Francisco, California; Mrs. René d'Harnoncourt, Washington, D. C.; Mrs. Charles Dietrich, Santa Fé, New Mexico; Mr. and Mrs. Kenneth B. Disher, Newton Highlands, Massachusetts; Mr. Frederic H. Douglas, Denver, Colorado; Mr. Charles de Young Elkus, San Francisco, California; Mrs. O. L. N. Foster, Denver, Colorado; Hon. Harold L. Ickes, Washington, D. C.; Dr. Ralph Linton, New York City; Mrs. Audrey McMahon, New York City; Mr. Earl Morris, Boulder, Colorado; Dr. Herbert J. Spinden, New York City; Mr. W. M. Tallant, Manatee, Florida; Miss Mary C. Wheelwright, Santa Fé, New Mexico; Miss Amelia Elizabeth White, Santa Fé, New Mexico; American Museum of Natural History, New York City; Brooklyn Museum, Brooklyn, New York; Buffalo Museum of Science, Buffalo, New York; Denver Art Museum, Denver, Colorado; Division of Exhibits, United States Department of the Interior, Washington, D. C.; Education Division, United States Indian Service, Washington, D. C.; Federal Arts Project, Utah W. P. A.; Federal Arts Project, New York W.P.A.; Field Museum of Natural History, Chicago, Illinois; Gila Pueblo, Globe, Arizona; Indian Arts and Crafts Board, Department of the Interior, Washington, D.C.; Laboratory of Anthropology, Santa Fé, New Mexico; Los Angeles Museum of History, Science, and Art, Los Angeles, California; Mesa Verde National Park, Colorado; Milwaukee Public Museum, Milwaukee, Wisconsin; Minnesota Historical Society, St. Paul, Minnesota; Montezuma Castle National Monument, Arizona; Museum of the American Indian, Heye Foundation, New York City; Museum of the Department of American Archaeology, Phillips Academy, Andover, Massachusetts; Museum of Modern Art, New York City; Museum of Navajo Ceremonial Art, Santa Fé, New Mexico; New York Historical Society, New York City; Ohio State Museum, Columbus, Ohio; Oklahoma Historical Society, Oklahoma City, Oklahoma; Peabody Museum of Archaeology and Ethnology, Harvard University, Cambridge, Massachusetts; Philbrook Museum, Tulsa, Oklahoma; Shiloh National Military Park, Pittsburgh Landing, Tennessee; Taylor Museum, Colorado Springs, Colorado; University of Alabama, Tuscaloosa, Alabama; University of Arkansas, Fayetteville, Arkansas; University of California Museum, Berkeley, California; University of Colorado Museum, Boulder, Colorado; University of Oklahoma, Norman, Oklahoma; University of Pennsylvania Museum, Philadelphia, Pennsylvania; University of Tennessee, Knoxville, Tennessee; Washington State Museum, Seattle, Washington.

On behalf of the Commissioners of the Indian Arts and Crafts Board of the United States Department of the Interior and of the President and the Trustees of the Museum of Modern Art, the directors of the exhibit wish to extend thanks to the following persons:

For Information and Counsel: Miss Katherine Bartlett; Dr. Franz Boas; Mr. J. O. Brew; Dr. Ruth Bunzel; Mr. E. K. Burnett; Dr. Douglas Byers; Mr. Holger Cahill, Mr. Kenneth M. Chapman; Mr. Henry B. Collins, Jr.; Dr. Frederica de Laguna; Mr. G. T. Emmons; Dr. Erna Gunther; Mr. Albert G. Heath; Dr. George Heye; Mr. Herbert W. Krieger; Dr. A. L. Kroeber; Dr. T. M. N. Lewis; Dr. Ralph Linton; Mr. Kenneth B. Miller; Dr. Richard Morgan; Miss Frances Raynolds; Dr. Frank H. H. Roberts, Jr.; Mr. Hugo Rodeck; Dr. Frank Setzler; Mr. Watson Smith; Dr. Frank G. Speck; Dr. Herbert J. Spinden; Mr. Alex Spoehr; Dr. Julian Steward; Mr. Matthew W. Stirling; Mr. Stanley Stubbs; Dr. John R. Swanton; Dr. George C. Vaillant; Miss H. Newell Wardle; Mr. Don Watson; Dr. Waldo Wedel, Miss Bella Weitzner.

For Organization of Research Work in the Field: Mr. Kenneth B. Disher.

For Collection of Data and Specimens: Mrs. Gwyneth B. Harrington; Miss Alice L. Marriott; Miss Gladys Tantaquidgeon.

For Supervision of the Installation of the Exhibit: Mr. Douglas Baxter.

For Supervision of Work on the Pictograph Replica and Making of Pictorial Maps: Mr. Elzy Bird; Mr. Basil Yurchenco.

For Preparation of Scale Drawings of Awatovi Murals: Miss Penrose Davis; Mr. Watson Smith.

For Basic Layout of the Book: Mrs. Lisa Foss.

For Assistance in Preparation of the Book: Mrs. H. B. Dillehunt, Jr.; Miss Anne Harding; Mrs. C. S. Hartman; Mrs. Arthur Kent; Mrs. Randall Provost; Miss Carol W. Rothschild; Miss Anne Stevens; Miss Bonnie Young.

Foreword

THE WHITE HOUSE

WASHINGTON, D. C.

At this time, when America is reviewing its cultural resources, this book and the exhibit on which it is based open up to us age-old sources of ideas and forms that have never been fully appreciated. In appraising the Indian's past and present achievements, we realize not only that his heritage constitutes part of the artistic and spiritual wealth of this country, but also that the Indian people of today have a contribution to make toward the America of the future.

In dealing with Indian art of the United States, we find that its sources reach far beyond our borders, both to the north and to the south. Hemispheric interchange of ideas is as old as man on this continent. Long before Columbus, tribes now settled in Arizona brought traditions to this country that were formed in Alaska and Canada; Indian traders from the foot of the Rocky Mountains exchanged goods and ideas with the great civilizations two thousand miles south of the Rio Grande. Related thoughts and forms that are truly of America are found from the Andes to the Mississippi Valley.

We acknowledge here a cultural debt not only to the Indians of the United States but to the Indians of both Americas.

ELEANOR ROOSEVELT

Introduction

TRIBAL TRADITIONS AND PROGRESS

For centuries the white man has taken advantage of the practical contributions made by the American Indian to civilization. Corn, one of the food staples most widely used today, was developed thousands of years ago through the diligence and patience of Indian agriculturists. Tomatoes, squash, potatoes and tobacco were cultivated on this continent long before the white man's arrival. In fact, the white invader was only too glad to learn from the Indian how to utilize the material resources of this country and adopted many of the native methods for his own use.

In spite of this ready recognition of the material achievements of the various Indian tribes, we have hardly ever stopped to ask what values there may be in Indian thought and art. An almost childish fascination with our own mechanical advancement has made us scorn the cultural achievements of all people who seem unable or unwilling to follow our rapid strides in the direction of what we believe to be the only worth-while form of progress.

For four centuries the Indians of the United States were exposed to the onslaught of the white invader, and military conquest was followed everywhere by civilian domination. As war never encourages objective appreciation of cultural values in the enemy camp, it is not surprising that in the days of the Indian wars tribal traditions were regarded as contemptibly backward. But it is deplorable that the advent of civilian domination added actual suppression to scorn. This destructive attitude of the civil authorities was rarely due to hostility. In many cases it was simply the result of their complete lack of understanding of Indian life, and sometimes it was even a manifestation of misguided good will. Indian tradition was seen as an obstacle to progress and every available means was employed to destroy it thoroughly and forever. Dances and ceremonials were outlawed, arts and crafts were decried as shameful survivals of a barbaric age and even the use of Indian languages was prohibited in many schools.

Only in recent years has it been realized that such a policy was not merely a violation of intrinsic human rights but was actually destroying values which could never be replaced, values so deeply rooted in tribal life that they are a source of strength for future generations. In recognition of these facts, the present administration is now cooperating with the various tribes in their efforts to preserve and develop those spiritual and artistic values in Indian tradition that the tribes consider essential. At the same time, the administration makes every effort to help them realize their desire to adopt from the white man such achievements as will make it possible for them to live successfully in a modern age. This attitude led to the promulgation of the Indian

Reorganization Act of 1934, which created a legal basis for the rehabilitation of Indian economic and cultural life. By this Act we are taking into consideration for the first time the validity of Indian tradition as well as the need for progress.

It is impossible to generalize on the present status of tribal tradition in the various groups. Some of them are still guided by tradition in all their activities and regard it as the basis of their entire economic, social and ceremonial life. Others have adopted some of the white man's ways, and some preserve tradition only in such subtle aspects of their culture that its existence is often imperceptible to the casual observer. It is also frequently true that factions within a tribe represent various attitudes ranging from strict adherence to open defiance of it. However, it must be said that Indian tradition still permeates in varying degrees every tribal unit that has not been completely absorbed by its white neighbors.

The survival of tribal cultures through generations of persecution and suppression is in itself a testimony to their strength and vitality. It is natural that a new appreciation of these values by the authorities and by part of the American public is now bringing to light in many places traditional customs and traditional thinking that have lived for years carefully shielded from unsympathetic eyes.

But our new willingness to recognize the value of Indian traditional achievement is unfortunately sometimes fostered by sentimentality rather than by true appreciation. There are people who have created for themselves a romantic picture of a glorious past that is often far from accurate. They wish to see the living Indian return to an age that has long since passed and they resent any change in his art. But these people forget that any culture that is satisfied to copy the life of former generations has given up hope as well as life itself. The fact that we think of Navaho silversmithing as a typical Indian art and of the horsemanship of the Plains tribes as a typical Indian characteristic proves sufficiently that those tribes were strong enough to make such foreign contributions entirely their own by adapting them to the pattern of their own traditions. Why should it be wrong for the Indian people of today to do what they have done with great success in the past? Invention or adaptation of new forms does not necessarily mean repudiation of tradition but is often a source of its enrichment.

To rob a people of tradition is to rob it of inborn strength and identity. To rob a people of opportunity to grow through invention or through acquisition of values from other races is to rob it of its future.

This publication, as well as the exhibition upon which it is based, aims to show that the Indian artist of today, drawing on the strength of his tribal tradition and utilizing the resources of the present, offers a contribution that should become an important factor in building the America of the future.

INDIAN ART

The Indian art of the United States is part of the larger body of native art produced in all the Americas. Indian culture reached its climax in the densely settled sections of Mexico and Central America, and in the Andean regions of South America. Large numbers of specialists provided the complex and highly developed native society of these regions with an infinite variety of decorated artifacts created to meet the demand of all classes from nobility to peasantry.

Compared with the art of these countries, that north of the Rio Grande could be described as provincial. It was produced on a relatively small scale and it never included such complicated processes of manufacture as metal casting or welding, which were perfectly mastered in the cultural centers south of the Rio Grande. At its best, however, it equals these arts in aesthetic refinement and often excels in freshness and power.

In theory, it should be possible to arrive at a satisfactory aesthetic evaluation of the art of any group without being much concerned with its cultural background. A satisfactory organization of lines, spaces, forms, shades and colors should be self-evident wherever we find it. Yet we know that increased familiarity with the background of an object not only satisfies intellectual curiosity but actually heightens appreciation of its aesthetic values.

This may be partly due to the fact that the eye, trained to see only familiar elements of form and color, actually fails to see in a work of foreign origin certain elements that may be of great importance to its maker. But surely it is also the result of a human inability to isolate aesthetic enjoyment, to separate it from habitually emotional or intellectual associations with specific forms or subjects. Only with knowledge of the background of a work of art are we able to synchronize, in effect, our pattern of associations with those of the culture that produced it and thus see it clearly enough to judge its merit. In looking at Indian objects it is essential to realize, for instance, how few of the frequent distortions or exaggerations of human or animal likenesses are meant to be grotesque. Most of them are the result of a consistent use of stylized tribal designs in the portrayal of living creatures. The Tlinkit mask, for example (Fig. 1), is a representation of a hawk that appears to us grotesque because it combines human features with a hawk's beak, an accepted practice in Northwest Coast art. The seemingly sinister expression of the eyes is due to a typical regional form of conventionalization. The Seneca mask (Fig. 2), on the other hand, was actually intended to create fear. It was made to represent the bodiless, floating head of a malevolent spirit.

Another example of misinterpretation of the Indian artist's motives for choosing certain forms is the popular belief that the strange double animals seen so frequently in Northwest Coast art were made to represent mythical monsters. Actually they are just a representation of the two sides of one and the same animal, and illustrate a tendency toward realism, not a desire to express

Fig. 1. Tlinkit hawk mask of painted wood, Alaska. Collection of Walter Waters, Wrangell, Alaska.

Fig. 2. Seneca spirit mask of painted wood, state of New York. Indian Arts and Crafts Board, Washington, D. C.

mystic powers. The Northwest Coast people always considered all aspects of their model, and used this device to give a complete rendering of their subject when they portrayed it on a two-dimensional plane (Fig. 3).

Our tendency to deal with unfamiliar manifestations of other cultures by describing them with one ambiguous and usually somewhat derogatory term is quite unfortunate. It is very misleading to refer to Indian art as primitive art. The word *primitive*, in either its literal sense, describing an early stage of development, or its popular sense, implying lack of refinement, only fits certain of the rudimentary and archaic forms of Indian art which can hardly be considered representative. Most Indian art is the result of a long period of development in which capable craftsmen devoted all their inventive skill to perfecting specialized techniques and styles. Some of it reaches a level that compares favorably with the products of any of the great pre-mechanic civilizations.

Traditional Indian art can best be considered as *folk art* because it is always an inextricable part of all social, economic and ceremonial activities of a given society. It creates within a collectively established scope of forms and patterns, and always serves a definite utilitarian or spiritual purpose that is accepted by the entire group.

Among certain groups, such as the Pueblo, centuries of rigidly organized collective activities have produced sharply defined collective concepts and art styles. Most subjects have prescribed conventionalized forms, and the same combinations of form elements occur over and over again with minor variations. In this type of culture the contribution of the individual artist is almost entirely limited to arrangement of patterns and to sensitive execution.

Such limitations are not, of course, considered a hardship by the traditional Pueblo artist, who is himself part of the group and whose concepts are therefore identical with those held by his tribe. The variety in quality found in Pueblo art

is convincing evidence that even the most rigidly established tribal patterns allow for individual achievement
of the highest degree.

Among other Indian cultures the established scope of
tribal art forms is considerably wider and allows in some
cases for a variety of renderings and arrangements that
is astonishing. How important it is for the Indian artist
to stay within the scope of his traditional arts, no matter
how wide or narrow that may be, can be learned from
his own judgment of tribal work, frequently rendered in
the terms of "right" or "wrong" instead of our customary "good" or "bad."

Fine art in the sense of art for art's sake is a concept
that is almost unknown in Indian cultures. There are
very few aboriginal art forms that have no established
function in tribal life. Some of the miniature ivory carvings of the Eskimo may be an exception to the rule since
there is no evidence that they serve any specific purpose,

Fig. 3. Haida design, representing
a killer whale, showing both sides
of the body.

but by and large every product made by an Indian artist has a function and is created by him
primarily to serve a given end. Artistic merit is simply considered a necessary by-product of good
workmanship.

The close relationship between aesthetic and technical perfection gives the work of most Indian
artists a basic unity rarely found in the products of an urban civilization. The perfection of
manufacturing processes in our own world has made it possible for us to force almost any raw
material into any given shape—an achievement that has turned out to be of doubtful value in the
hands of many ambitious but undiscriminating contemporaries. The Indian artist, whose simple
tools have always forced him to study his raw material in order to discover just what treatment
will best utilize its inherent characteristics, has developed a sense of the fitness of form and material that gives distinction to all his work.

This sense of fitness and this close relationship between product and treatment are also apparent
in the Indian's choice of ornamentation for objects serving different purposes. Baskets and pottery
vessels that are not meant to be seen in motion are generally decorated with asymmetric or organic
designs that give them a life of their own. Fabrics and hides used for clothing, however, are more
often ornamented with geometric and bilaterally symmetric patterns, since they receive their
motion from the body of the wearer. The embroidered sash and the pottery vessel reproduced in

Fig. 4. Embroidered Hopi sash, Arizona. Lent by the Denver Art Museum, Denver.

Figures 4 and 5 show this differentiation in products of the Pueblo area.

Much has been said and more has been written about symbolism in Indian art. It is true that symbolism has always had an important part in Indian culture and in the formulation of Indian design styles. But it is often difficult to trace and is much misunderstood. The word *symbol* has always had a great appeal to buyers of Indian curios, who love to think that they can purchase a mystery and a half with every souvenir. This public demand for symbols has so overstimulated the fertile imagination of eager salesmen that today the word is frequently used as if it were a synonym for Indian design.

Actually, symbols were and still are used in most Indian civilizations both to convey abstract concepts and to record facts. In the first case they have, as a rule, the ceremonial content so often associated with the word, while in the latter case they simply represent a form of picture-writing. But the meaning of given symbols is hardly ever the same in different tribes and cannot be interpreted without a comprehensive knowledge of the circumstances under which they were used. In some tribes their meaning changes from family to family or even from individual to individual. In groups that have a very formalized religious system the same symbols are used rather consistently, while in others their meaning may change from one occasion to another. Many designs created originally as symbols have later on been widely used simply as decorative devices, and many decorative elements have been given symbolic meaning by their makers at certain times.

In many tribes it is customary to give to specific designs names that are either descriptive or simply used as a means of identification. This custom has further obscured an already complicated problem, since it is frequently difficult to know if a word associated with a given design designates the design itself or refers to its symbolic content.

It is impossible here to go into more detail on this involved subject. Suffice it to say that only the meaning given to a design by its maker transforms it into a symbol, and that it is therefore impossible to interpret specific symbols without a knowledge of their origin in each case.

Beyond such general statements little can be said about Indian art that would fit all the various tribes and tribal groups, since each area of Indian culture has an art of its own. Indian art always

Fig. 5. Pottery jar from Acoma Pueblo. Lent by the Laboratory of Anthropology, Santa Fé, New Mexico.

was and still is regional in the deepest sense of the word. The artists of the Northwest Coast not only portray men and animals of that region but also convey in form and design the very essence of the gloomy fog-bound coast with its dark forests and its mysterious animation. Even the Pueblo potter, whose most abstract forms abstain completely from representation, still achieves effects in color and design that are essentially of the Southwest and could not be associated with any other part of the country. Indian art from coast to coast actually recreates the land, America, in every one of its countless variations.

INDIAN ORIGINS AND HISTORY

Asia is the place of origin of all North and South American Indians. The very close physical relationship of Indians and northern Asiatics and the lack of any traces of very ancient man in the Americas show clearly that the Indians are relatively recent arrivals of Asiatic origin.

The entry into America was made from Siberia across Bering Strait into Alaska. The most widely accepted theory is that the migrations began fifteen to twenty thousand years ago, after the glaciers of the last Ice Age had receded sufficiently to allow passage, and continued until perhaps three thousand years ago. There is some possibility that there were slight migrations at an earlier period, probably about forty thousand years ago. No evidence has been found of pre-historic migrations from Europe or of mass migrations by canoe from the Pacific Islands.

A study of their physical structure proves that the Indians are mixed racially and were so before they came to America. Even the ancient remains show relationships with the physical types of the different divisions of mankind. The distribution of racial physical characteristics among Indians indicates that these people are basically Mongoloid with traces of intermixture which occurred in the remote past.

The study of Indian languages also makes it clear that different kinds of peoples were involved in the migrations. The hundreds of Indian tongues spoken today can be grouped into a small number of unrelated linguistic stocks, each presumably the speech of a distinct family of races.

The main line of travel during the migrations appears to have been from Bering Strait across the Rocky Mountains of northern Alaska to the more or less level country of northern Canada. From there the people spread out fan-like south along the eastern side of the Rocky Mountains and east toward the Atlantic. Some groups, however, moved south from Alaska through the mountains or along the Pacific coast. Many of the migrants passed down into South and Central America. At the time of the discovery of America, about one million Indians were very thinly scattered over the area north of Mexico. Vastly larger populations lived south of that line.

Very little is known about the Indians between their coming from Asia and their discovery by the Europeans, and the available dates are so scattered that a clear outline of the prehistoric phase of Indian life cannot yet be given. It must suffice to say that there were constant shiftings of location and of cultural developments, out of which finally emerged the specific historic cultures which are treated at more length in the section devoted to the living traditions.

To divide the story of a race into prehistoric and historic phases conforms with the accepted practice of anthropology, itself divided into archaeology, the study of prehistoric man, and ethnology, the study of historic and modern man. Such a division is useful but of necessity somewhat arbitrary, and should be adopted only after careful examination of its implications.

In its literal sense the historic period of a people starts with the appearance of the first methodic records of their life and activities, whether these records are made by the people themselves or by an outsider. Since the Indians living north of the Rio Grande were still illiterate at the time of their discovery by Europeans, our earliest records of them are those made by the explorers. These records date from widely different times for different groups. In New Mexico and on the Atlantic coast records are available from the beginning of the sixteenth century, whereas certain tribes in the West were not discovered and described until the nineteenth century.

The phrase *historic period* has also acquired a cultural meaning, implying a new stage of intellectual and technical development comparable with that of literate cultures. For the Indians north of Mexico, the beginning of the historic period in this cultural sense did not usually coincide with their first appearance in written records. If a tribe's first historian belonged to a white group that actually settled among the people, his first description was often closely followed by cultural change within the tribe caused by contacts with the settlers. But if he was an isolated explorer or if his group did not mingle with the tribe, the old life might survive for generations.

In some cases the beginning of the historic phase in the cultural sense actually preceded discovery. Certain Plains tribes, for example, had definitely abandoned the traditional primitive culture long before Lewis and Clark found them, because intertribal trade had brought them European products that changed their entire cultural pattern before they ever saw a white man.

The time needed for the transition from a prehistoric to a historic phase of a culture varies according to region. In the Pueblo area prehistory gave way to history very gradually, whereas in the Southeast the old Indian culture vanished almost overnight with the coming of Europeans.

This book and the exhibit which it describes are divided into three sections: prehistoric art, historic art or the living traditions, and Indian art for modern living. The terms *historic* and *prehistoric* are used here in the cultural sense, and late survivals of prehistoric styles are therefor included in the first section, even if they were actually made during historic periods. In the case of a civilization where the transition period was extraordinarily long, the division has had to be rather arbitrary. Prehistoric elements that have become an inextricable part of its historic picture are dealt with in the section devoted to the living traditions.

Color in Indian Art

A series of plates indicating the traditional range of color in Indian art.

Stone Pipe from Southeastern Alaska. 2¼″ long, 1½″ deep. Lent by the Museum of the American Indian, Heye Foundation, New York. (9286)

We know very little about painting among the early Northwest Coast people but their selection of jade and similar stones for carving reveals an interest in color and beautiful surfaces.

This serpentine pipe is a typical example of the animal sculpture of the region. Its style is reminiscent of early petroglyphs but we have no indication of its age. Collected about 1885 by G. T. Emmons at Kluckwan, Alaska.

Stone Pipe from Moundville, Alabama. 4″ high, 8½″ wide. Lent by the Museum of the American Indian, Heye Foundation, New York. (17/2810)

Some of the stone pipes found in the eastern United States are the finest examples of prehistoric human and animal representation north of the Rio Grande. This outstanding piece is made of porphyritic sandstone. Like the other so-called Great Pipes, its weight and size suggest that it was intended for ceremonial purposes. The importance of tobacco in both the everyday life and the rituals of the prehistoric eastern tribes can be judged from the large number of pipes of all types found throughout the area. This pipe was excavated by C. B. Moore.

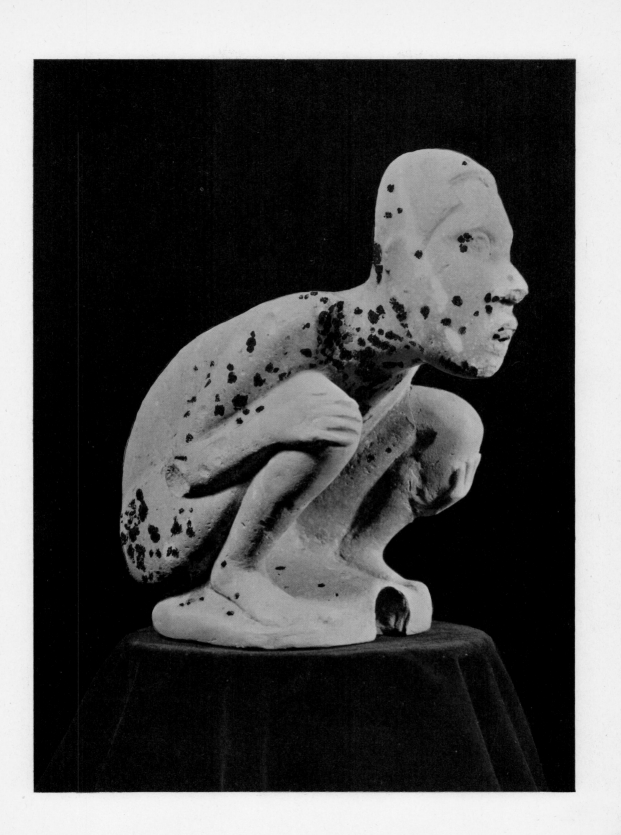

Painted Stone Mortar from Pueblo Bonito, New Mexico. 8½″ long, 5″ in diameter. Lent by the Museum of the American Indian, Heye Foundation, New York. (5/1364)

Prehistoric painted stone vessels from the Southwest are exceedingly rare and this mortar is the finest one known. Its designs are closely related to those found on painted or woven cotton textiles which in turn were derived from basketry patterns. This common origin of most ancient Pueblo design styles also influenced the decorations on pottery but only a few pieces have retained the character of the original woven pattern as fully as this mortar. Excavated about 1898 by G. H. Pepper.

Kiva Mural, Awatovi, Arizona. 120″ long, 50″ high. Lent by the Indian Arts and Crafts Board, United States Department of the Interior.

Large and elaborate murals have been discovered in recent years on the walls of kivas or ceremonial rooms in some of the prehistoric Pueblo ruins. The mural illustrated here was found in Awatovi in northeastern Arizona. It is a replica executed in the ancient manner by four contemporary Hopi artists, Fred K[...], Charles Loloma, Herbert Komoyousie and Victor Cootswytewa, whose ancestors painted the original. Since the original murals have disintegrated the artists based their work on scale drawings made during the excavations by staff members of the Peabody Museum in Cambridge. The original was excavated by J. O. Brew.

Pictographs of the Basketmaker Culture, Barrier Canyon, Utah. Kodachrome by Robert M. Jones, Utah Art Project, WPA.

The prehistoric Basketmakers of the Southwest often covered huge areas of the smooth sandstone walls of their desert canyons with paintings of tall, square-shouldered figures. Although some of the pictographs date from the early centuries of the Christian era, they are well preserved because of the extremely dry climate. The Great Gallery of Barrier Canyon, shown here in a photograph, has been reproduced in full size, 12½ feet by 60 feet, for the exhibition.

Pottery Jar, Acoma Pueblo, New Mexico. 11¾″ high, 12¾″ in diameter. Lent by the Denver Art Museum, Denver. (XAC-28-G)

Jars for carrying and storing water are the most common vessels made by Pueblo potters. Each village has developed one or more characteristic shapes decorated with certain favorite designs. On Acoma pottery the prevailing geometric figures are often supplemented by stylized parrots like the one illustrated here. The red and yellow paints are iron-stained earths. Made about 1900.

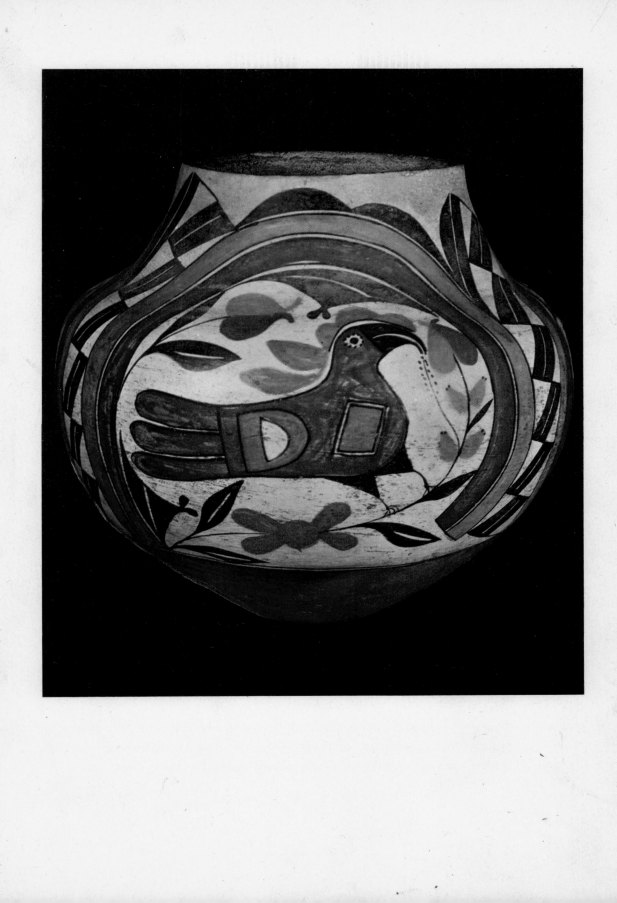

Navaho Sand Painting, Arizona. Reproduction lent by the Museum of Navajo Ceremonial Art, Santa Fé, New Mexico.

This sand painting representing the Sky Father and the Earth Mother is one of a series from the Shooting Chant, an important Navaho religious ceremony. Such paintings are made by sprinkling powdered colored rock and earth on a flat bed of sand, and are an integral part of many curing rites. They can be executed only under the direction of a medicine man and must be ceremonially destroyed before sundown of the day on which they were begun. The original of the one illustrated measured about 8 by 10 feet.

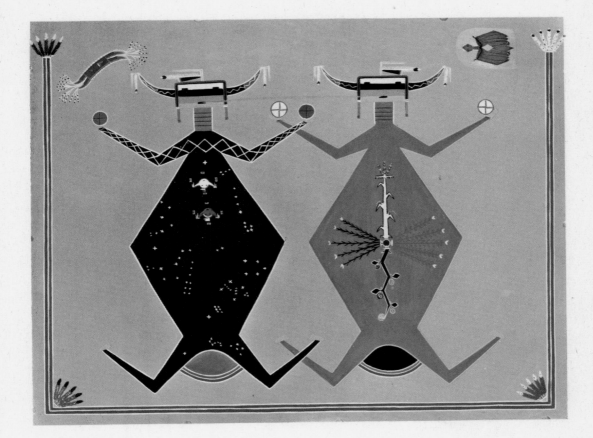

Painted Leather Poncho, Chiricahua Apache, Arizona. 46″ long, 31″ deep. Lent by the Museum of the American Indian, Heye Foundation, New York. (16/1349)

The main figures on this ceremonial skin garment represent gods, one of them flanked by two suns. Life forms in Apache painting are usually connected with the great powers of earth and sky from which the medicine men draw their magic strength.

The archaic forms and the nervous, angular outline of these paintings are unique with this tribe. This piece was collected by John G. Bourke.

Mohave Pottery Bottle, Southeast California. 9½″ high, 9¼″ in diameter. Lent by the Denver Art Museum, Denver. (XMo-1-66)

The art of the Desert Dwellers of southern Arizona and southern California is sober and restrained. Its geometric patterns decorate utilitarian baskets and pottery vessels of simple shape. Only among the Yuma and Mohave are found small clay images of striking savagery reminiscent of those left by the ancient inhabitants of the region. These images, ornamented with strings of colored beads, often appear on pottery bottles that conform in shape and design to the regional tradition. Collected about 1900 by Vroman.

Burden Basket, Pomo, West Central California. 26″ high, 25″ in diameter at top. Lent by the American Museum of Natural History, New York. (50/2600)

The Pomo are the best basketmakers in California, excelling all other tribes in perfection of technique and variety of type. This burden basket is made in a diagonal twined weave of light sedge root and dark redbud bark. It is carried on the back in a net passing around the shoulders.

The pattern is a classic example of the design style, based on triangles, which is so predominant in California. Collected in 1901 by C. F. Briggs at Ukiah.

Painted Elk Hide from the Central Plains. 77″ long, 70″ wide. Lent by Amelia Elizabeth White, Santa Fé, New Mexico.

Painting on skin was one of the outstanding art forms of the Plains Indians. It was practiced by both men and women, but in distinctive styles. From the making of historic records, such as winter counts and pictorial biographies, developed a representative art practiced exclusively by men. Painting by women was restricted to the geometric decoration of robes and rawhide articles.

The painting shown here depicts a buffalo hunt and the festivities connected with it. The paints are colored earths and the painting tool is a thin, spongy piece of buffalo knee bone.

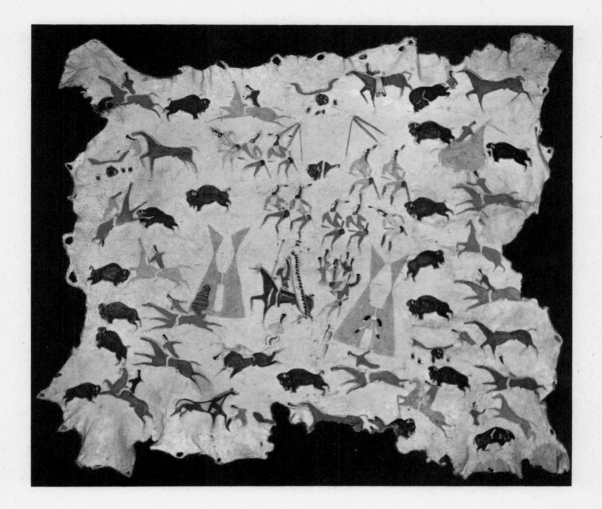

Porcupine Quill Embroidery, Delaware Tribe. 14½″ long, 7¼″ wide. Lent by the Museum of the American Indian, Heye Foundation, New York. (19/3264)

Quill work is the most distinctive of all Indian arts since it is done nowhere else in the world.

Because the technique of quill embroidery lends itself particularly to the making of geometric designs, animal representations are relatively scarce and usually conventionalized to become an integral part of a geometric allover pattern.

Before the introduction of commercial dyes, the most frequently used colors were the black and orange shown here. White is the natural color of the quill.

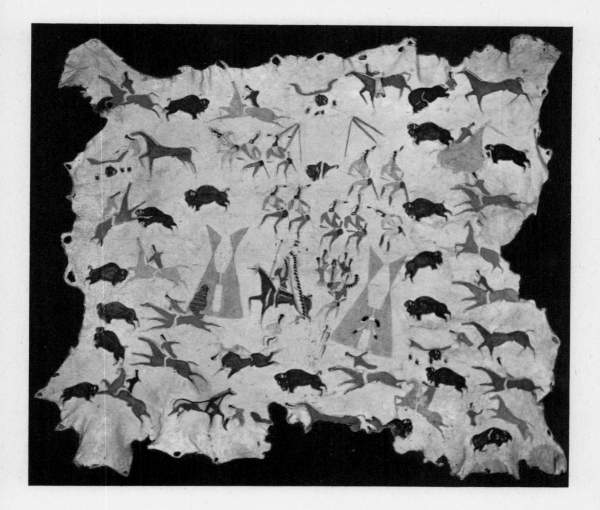

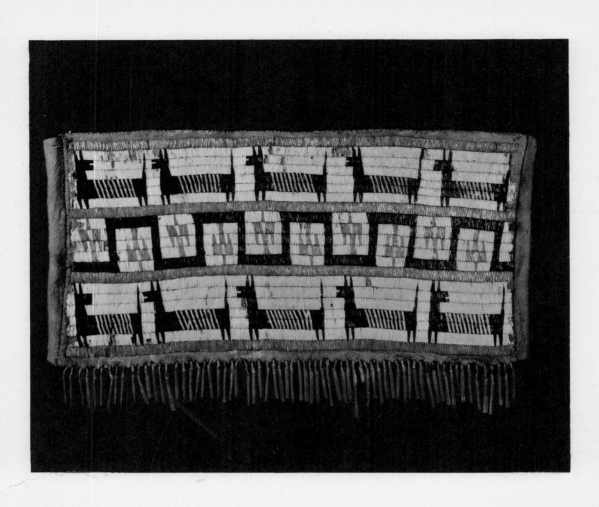

Headdress Ornament, Tsimshian, British Columbia. 7½" high. Lent by the Museum of the American Indian, Heye Foundation, New York. (1/4295)

The chiefs of the Northwest Coast tribes wore high cylindrical headdresses covered with ermine and surmounted by a crown of sea lion bristles. These headdresses were often decorated with wooden ornaments intricately carved and inlaid with abalone shell. The ornament illustrated here represents the beaver, one of the totemic animals most frequently used in Northwest Coast design. The carving was collected by G. T. Emmons at Kit-lagh-damoks village.

Wooden Mask, Eskimo, Southwest Alaska. 15″ long, 9″ wide. Lent by the University of California, Berkeley, California. (25854)

Eskimo masks showing extreme distortions are said to represent the spirits seen by medicine men. Mask making among the Eskimos is restricted to a relatively small area between the mouth of the Yukon River south to the Aleutian Peninsula.

The colors of this mask are typical of the Eskimo artists' preference for white backgrounds relieved by areas of gray, rose, red earth, and chalky greens or blues.

Color in Indian Art

Green Corn Ceremony. Gouache by Awa Tsireh. 27¾" long, 19½" high. Lent by the Museum of Modern Art, New York. (330.39)

Only in recent years have Indian artists produced paintings made for the sake of their decorative value alone. The new school of Indian painting was encouraged by white artists but takes its subject matter almost exclusively from Indian life and retains much of tribal tradition in concept and execution. Awa Tsireh of San Ildefonso Pueblo was one of the founders of this school in the Southwest.

Pawnee Ribbonwork Applied to Modern Evening Dress.

Silk ribbon appliqué work in traditional designs has been made by many tribes of the East, the Mississippi Valley and the Great Lakes region since this material was first made available to them in the eighteenth century. The type of ribbon applied to this dress is made for trimming blankets. Narrower strips are used for leggings and moccasin flaps. The dress was designated by F. A. Picard for the Indian Arts and Crafts Board to show the adaptability of original Indian work to modern fashions.

Prehistoric Art: Introduction

Our knowledge of Indian prehistory in the United States, Canada and Alaska is quite limited and scattered. We know most about the Southwest, where the various culture areas can be most clearly traced and where an accurate system of dating sites and remains has been established through the use of the tree ring calendar described on page 100.

In the eastern half of the United States the amount of archaeological material collected and examined is very considerable; but here lack of any practicable system of dating and a bewildering overlapping of cultural characteristics make it impossible at present to get a clear picture of developments. In the Plains and along the Pacific coast archaeological investigations have scarcely

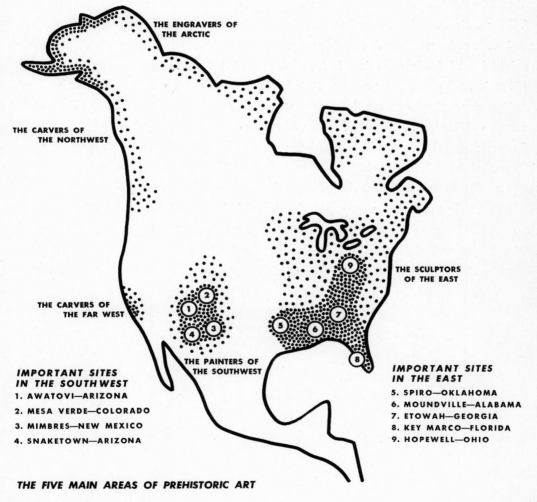

THE ENGRAVERS OF THE ARCTIC

THE CARVERS OF THE NORTHWEST

THE SCULPTORS OF THE EAST

THE CARVERS OF THE FAR WEST

THE PAINTERS OF THE SOUTHWEST

IMPORTANT SITES IN THE SOUTHWEST
1. AWATOVI—ARIZONA
2. MESA VERDE—COLORADO
3. MIMBRES—NEW MEXICO
4. SNAKETOWN—ARIZONA

IMPORTANT SITES IN THE EAST
5. SPIRO—OKLAHOMA
6. MOUNDVILLE—ALABAMA
7. ETOWAH—GEORGIA
8. KEY MARCO—FLORIDA
9. HOPEWELL—OHIO

THE FIVE MAIN AREAS OF PREHISTORIC ART

been started, and in Canada they have been limited for the most part to the southeastern section. In Alaska a few centers have been studied intensively but vast areas remain scientifically unknown.

In prehistoric times the entire territory stretching from the Rio Grande and the Gulf of Mexico north to the Arctic was only sparsely settled. The population of what is now the United States consisted of hundreds of more or less scattered tribes belonging to many racial and linguistic families. All these tribes at one time or another reached a level of culture at which they were able to manufacture simple tools of stone and bone. There are indications that rough basketry was produced nearly everywhere from coast to coast, and crude pottery has been found in most of the area except along the Pacific between San Diego and southwestern Alaska. The products common to the entire area were not necessarily similar in appearance, but they were almost uniform in the limited degree of their development.

What we shall consider, therefore, in this book, is a broad level of very simple technical and artistic efforts. From this basis certain groups of prehistoric people advanced at different times to much higher levels of production. In fact, it is possible today to designate five distinct sectors of prehistoric Indian art that progressed far beyond primitive efforts. The regions where these developments took place were the eastern woodland area of the United States, the Southwest, southern California, southeastern Alaska and northern Alaska (page 49).

In considering the general level and the five areas of high development, we must bear in mind that our judgment is based solely on the prehistoric artifacts that have survived. There is always the possibility that groups other than those of the five important areas may have produced objects of distinction, but that these were made of such perishable materials that they disintegrated with time and are therefore lost to us. It is also possible that areas relatively primitive in their material culture may have had a high culture along non-material lines.

A study of objects found in the five advanced areas shows that each area preferred certain techniques of manufacture and had a predominant interest in form, space or line. The prehistoric people of the Southwest, for example, excelled in two-dimensional decoration on a great variety of surfaces. Their skill as creators of pottery shapes is undeniable, but the painted decoration on their ware is rarely subordinated to the form of the vessel and usually constitutes its most important feature. This interest in two-dimensional design is also evident in their murals, textile patterns and basketry. Even their polychrome carving is often primarily a group of planes arranged to receive color patterns.

In the entire eastern sector, from the Mississippi basin to the Atlantic, the majority of objects found reveals a strong feeling for three-dimensional form. Sculpture in stone occurs frequently and pottery was produced in an astounding variety of skillfully modeled shapes. Engraved and, to a lesser extent, painted decorations appear on many pieces but these decorations are not so much an end in themselves as a means of stressing the shape of the vessel.

Findings in northern Alaska consist mostly of small ivory objects. They show a subtle feeling for form but are differentiated from all other prehistoric artifacts by an emphasis on line decoration. The people who lived south of the Eskimo region, along the coast of Alaska and British Columbia, carved in both stone and wood, but it is their massive stone dishes, weapons and ceremonial objects that are best known to us. The smallest group is the one in southern California, where both wood and stone carving were done in simple but effective forms.

Since the surviving artifacts in these five areas point to the existence of such distinct preferences and abilities among the little-known people who made them, it seems reasonable to call the different groups by names which a study of the artifacts suggests. We therefore call the first group mentioned the Painters of the Southwest, the others the Sculptors of the East, the Engravers of the Arctic, the Carvers of the Northwest and the Carvers of the Far West.

Though each group preferred specific art forms, all groups made use of certain basic techniques. People of all the areas worked whatever solid materials were at hand by chipping, rubbing or cutting. Stone was the most usual material, followed in order of frequency by bone, wood, shell and metal. The work ranged in skill from the crudest kind of pecking or abrading through fine implement-making to true sculpture. The tribes of the Mississippi basin were the outstanding sculptors. Sculpture was also produced in the Southwest, southern California, and on the Northwest Coast, but these regions were both less prolific and less significant. Copper work was done only east of the Mississippi and no other metals were used.

The two great pottery regions were east of the Mississippi and in the Southwest, although some pottery was also made in the extreme southern part of California and on the Plains.

Because of the perishable nature of the materials, it has been impossible to trace the full distribution of weaving and basketry. These two crafts reached brilliant heights in the Southwest but elsewhere, as far as we can tell, were undistinguished although fairly common.

In the matter of design styles, the differences between the five areas are very striking. There never has been such a thing as one Indian design style common to all groups in the United States. The style characteristic of each prehistoric area was based on the use of specific design elements, usually simple geometric figures. The map on page 52 shows the distribution of these design elements, while the illustrations below it show how they were applied to actual objects.

The Sculptors of the East emphasized the shapes of their stone and pottery pieces with fine linear designs of two major types: in the northern area most designs were based on the use of parallel lines, in the south the spiral was the most frequently used element. These styles are both extinct and have been replaced by new ones introduced during the colonial period.

The Painters of the Southwest, who preferred spatial rather than linear design, had a special liking for painted areas defined by right angles. Since textiles and basketry were among the earliest products of this people, it is quite possible that their preference for right angles originated in the technique of weaving, where the crossing of warp and weft makes the use of rectangular design almost inescapable. The rectangular style of decoration is most frequently found in their painted pottery. It was used most consistently in the northern and central sections. In the south the rigid geometric patterns are sometimes supplemented by curved lines and organic figures.

The stone carvings of the Northwest Coast and of California, which frequently took the form of living beings, have little surface decoration except that necessary to indicate the anatomy of the subject, but in each area there is nevertheless a definite regional style.

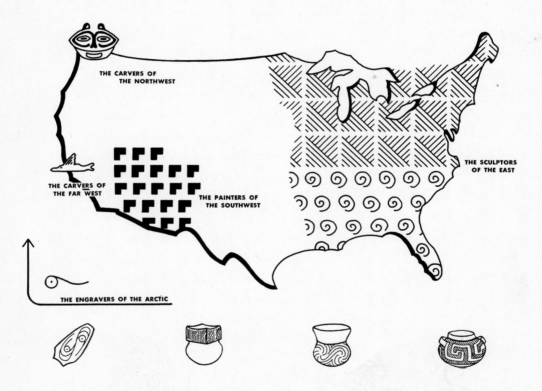

Fig. 7. Distribution of basic design elements in prehistoric art, and examples of their application. The figures below the map are, from left to right, an ivory object from Alaska, an Iroquois jar from New York State, a clay vessel from Arkansas and a jar from Arizona.

52   *Prehistoric Art: Introduction*

The Carvers of the Far West

In recent years there have been discovered in three counties of southern California a few carved stone, shell and wood objects, the artistic merit of which rises far above the average level of prehistoric California crafts. In contrast with the great size of other areas of Indian artistic production, the region which produced these carvings is extremely small.

Fortunately, much was written about these tribes by early explorers. Their discoverer, Rodriguez Cabrillo, kept a diary of his expedition in 1542. Nearly two hundred years later Father Boscana carefully recorded many details of their lives.

Fig. 8. Area inhabited by the ancient Carvers of the Far West.

By adding the results of modern excavations to such early accounts, a quite well-rounded picture of these Carvers of the Far West can be recreated. There were two groups of them: the Chumash of the Hokan linguistic family, and three members of the Uto-Aztecan family—the Gabrielino, the Fernandeno and the Juaneno—who were named after the Spanish missions with which they were connected. The Chumash lived in the Santa Barbara region and the others in the neighborhood of Los Angeles. The offshore Channel Islands, of which Santa Catalina is the best known, were divided between the two groups.

Most of the life of these Indians was passed on or near the mainland shore or on the islands. Though their territory stretched inland to the coast range of mountains, the back country was less densely populated than the coast. It was used mainly as a source of food supplies, such as game, acorns and wild plant seeds eaten to supplement the sea foods on which the people principally lived. Dwellings were light huts of poles thatched with grass. Little clothing was needed

Fig. 9. Gabrielino soapstone figurines from Los Angeles County, California. Left, a swordfish. 7″ long. Right, a sailfish. 11⅝″ long. Lent by the Museum of the American Indian, Heye Foundation, New York. (20/990 and 20/1854)

because of the mild climate. The men wore nothing, and the women short back and front aprons of deerskin. In cold weather coarsely woven robes of fur or feathers were worn. Women sometimes wore a close fitting basket cap.

The high degree of technical and manual skill attained by these people in their manufactures placed them in a class above that of other California Indians and inspired enthusiastic comments from early explorers. Especially praised were the seagoing canoes made of handhewn planks sewn together with sinew cords and calked with asphalt. No other Indians made canoes in such a technically advanced manner. Soapstone vessels, figurines and clubs are the most developed technically of the Chumash and Gabrielino artifacts which have been found. Vessels for household use are massive, almost globular jars very symmetrically rounded and smoothly polished. A few have simple geometric carved designs near the rim. Certain jars are more elaborate and may have been used in connection with the religious use of toloache, a narcotic drink made from Jimson weed. These jars often have designs made of shell beads inlaid in asphalt (Fig. 10). The figurines are very simplified representations of sea creatures, which by their smoothly flowing lines suggest swift and easy motion (Fig. 9). These carvings clearly served no utilitarian purpose and, since some of them suggest characters in the religion and mythology of the people, it seems likely that they had some ritualistic use.

The few wooden carvings which have survived the destructive effects of the moist climate show

Fig. 10. A Gabrielino soapstone jar inlaid with shell beads from Los Angeles County, California. 11″ high, 10″ in diameter. Lent by the Museum of the American Indian, Heye Foundation, New York. (19/1615)

workmanship as fine as that of the stone carvings. Old records speak of well-made wooden bowls inlaid with abalone shell, but none exists today. From abalone shells they also made heavy curved fishhooks of graceful shape. Clam shells were made into the disk-shaped beads used as money by all the southern California tribes.

Like so many other Indian tribes of southern California, the Chumash and Gabrielino were gathered around the Spanish missions in the late eighteenth century. Though their relationship with the missionaries was unusually friendly, the Indians could not adjust themselves to the new civilization. They fell more and more into a state of mental and spiritual depression which expressed itself in widespread abortion. By the early nineteenth century their numbers were rapidly diminishing, and now only a few mixed bloods remain of the thousands who once swarmed over the beaches and islands.

Prehistoric Art: The Carvers of the Far West

The Carvers of the Northwest Coast

Prehistory ended late on the Northwest Coast. Not until 1774 did exploration by white men begin and many sections of the vast tangled wilderness remained unknown till well into the nineteenth century.

The study of Northwest prehistory has received little attention. Elsewhere in North America, archaeologists have been digging into the past for several generations so that the story of antiquity is quite well known in some sections. But in the Northwest, investigation has been limited to the extreme northern and southern ends of the long narrow strip of coast stretching from the state of Washington to Alaska. Of the hundreds of miles between these two extremes we know nothing except what can be gleaned from native traditions and occasional pictures carved on rocks.

From these petroglyphs it can be seen that the characteristic animal art, which was to develop so brilliantly in the nineteenth century, existed before the period of discovery. We know also from the late eighteenth century writings and collections of Captain Cook and his contemporaries that the sculpture, weaving and architecture so typical of the region were already developed in their time to a point which suggests ancient beginnings.

From a study of these early written records and of the few known ancient specimens, and from investigations of modern tribes, it is possible to discern the rough outlines of a picture of the past.

A good many centuries ago people from the interior spread out to the coast in southern British Columbia and possibly northwestern Washington. Enough knowledge of these people and their artifacts has been gained from excavations to

Fig. 11. Area inhabited by the ancient Carvers of the Northwest Coast.

Fig. 12. A Haida limestone head with eyes of iridescent abalone shell, from British Columbia. 5½″ long, 2″ wide, 1¼″ deep. Lent by the American Museum of Natural History, New York. 16/IA(629)

make it clear that they were not the same as the tribes to the north. The more northern groups emerged from Alaska at a late date and pressed south along the coast till they met the already established tribes first mentioned. It was the art of the newcomers that used the animal forms so typical of the region. There are indications that these migrants from the North may have made the crossing from Siberia at a relatively late period. Unfortunately, there is slight chance of finding much concrete evidence through excavation, for the combination of a damp climate and a material culture based on wood and other perishable substances does not make for a lasting record of the past.

All remains of northwestern prehistory which have been found are stone or bone, shell or antler. Most of them are undecorated tools, but some are carved into shapes which anticipate the development of the elaborate art of the nineteenth century. In these pieces the use of living forms and the eccentric curve, both basic in northwestern art, are very evident.

Though native copper existed, it was too soft for tools. Hence all carving had to be done with stone blades. Fortunately jade was available for this purpose, the only jade north of Mexico. It came from southwestern British Columbia and was worked into smoothly polished adze blades, knives and chisels.

There are no indications that Indian life on the Northwest Coast was basically very different in prehistoric times from that of the early nineteenth century. The ancient art of this region was certainly less elaborate and probably less diversified than that of the historic period, but its basic concepts and form elements are still used today.

Fig. 13. A stone totem pole from Vancouver Island. 2' 1½" high, 5¼" wide at base. Lent by the Royal Ontario Museum of Archaeology, Ottawa, Canada.

Prehistoric Art: The Carvers of the Northwest Coast

The Engravers of
the Arctic

The beginning of Eskimo history in America is as yet unknown, though it now seems certain that the race arrived on this continent several thousand years ago. Full details of the time and circumstances of its coming will not be clear until many more excavations have been made in the thousands of miles of Eskimo territory between Siberia and eastern Greenland. That such details may eventually be known is not unlikely, for the frozen soil of the Arctic preserves the relics of man's past remarkably well.

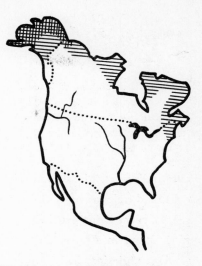

Fig. 14. Area inhabited by the ancient Engravers of the Arctic.

Ancient Eskimo remains have been discovered in several sites in the Arctic including the islands in or near Bering Strait, various spots in eastern Siberia, the neighborhood of Point Barrow, Alaska, the Hudson Bay region and Greenland. Though they differ greatly in detail there is a fundamental similarity which binds them together, showing that the Eskimo of antiquity, like those of today, belonged to one of the great cultural divisions of mankind and constituted a single basic physical type.

In the Arctic there is no definite break between archaeology and ethnology, the past merging imperceptibly into the present. This is not surprising when one realizes that conditions in the Far North have changed hardly at all for thousands of years. With a few exceptions the same wild life, on which human life depends, has always existed. Only slight fluctuations of climate

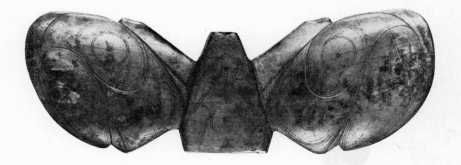

Fig. 15. Ivory carving, of unknown use, Old Bering Sea style. Found in Siberia. 8⅜″ long, 2¹³⁄₁₆″ wide, 1⅛″ thick. Lent by the University of Pennsylvania Museum, Philadelphia. (NA4254)

Fig. 16. An engraved ivory harpoon point from Banks Island, Alaska. 3¾" long. Lent by the Museum of the American Indian, Heye Foundation, New York. (2/4327)

have occurred. Above all, the remoteness of the Eskimo from civilization has kept from them most of those influences which have broken the link between present and past in the case of other native races.

The ancient Eskimo were great makers of tools and hunting and fishing equipment. Since walrus ivory provided them with a material ideally suited to the making of fine durable implements, its decoration became their outstanding art. The smooth surface of polished ivory and the small size of the objects themselves led to a development of delicate line-engraving that is unsurpassed on the continent.

Like every living art theirs was flexible and passed through many related phases. The earliest work found in Alaska is decorated with gracefully curving lines which subtly emphasize the smallest variations in the form of the object. The flow of these lines is punctuated by dotted circles that clarify the composition. The animal head in Figure 17 is a good example of this type of engraving. It belongs to the Old Bering Sea style, one of the great native styles of America, from which evolved the art of the Punuk period. This period is characterized by an increasing tendency toward the use of straight lines and by a less highly developed technical perfection. It is remarkable that the deterioration of the technique in the Punuk period coincided with the introduction of iron from Asia approximately one thousand years ago.

The Punuk style was in turn ancestral to modern Eskimo art, which is treated in detail on page 185.

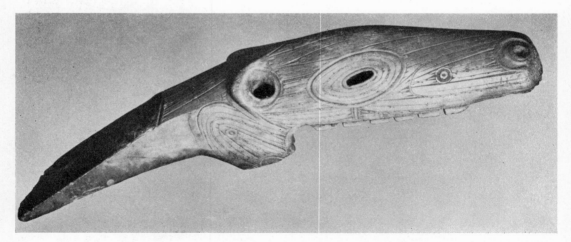

Fig. 17. Ivory drum handle carved to represent a bear's head. The engraving is of the Old Bering Sea type. Little Diomede Island, Alaska. 5⅝" long. Lent by the Museum of the American Indian, Heye Foundation, New York. (18/8622)

The Sculptors of the East

In prehistoric times there lived in the eastern United States a large number of tribes who were united in the field of art by their common interest in three-dimensional form. This interest manifested itself in true sculpture in wood and stone, in a vast variety of pottery shapes and in an emphasis on outlines that suggest plastic form even in flat objects like those cut from mica or sheet copper (Fig. 19).

They lived in the entire eastern section of the United States, as shown in Figure 18. On the west the area included eastern Texas and Oklahoma, Missouri, eastern Iowa, and Wisconsin.

In the East, archaeology has been carried on much longer than anywhere else in the country. Thomas Jefferson was one of the earliest investigators. As a result of this century or more of study, a vast number of facts has been gathered. But, unfortunately for modern students, it is not easy to fit the accumulated data into any sort of clear pattern. The situation is extraordinarily complex. Three factors are chiefly responsible for this difficulty: the lack of any absolute dates; the small number of sites where it is possible to read the sequence of events by means of layers of cultural remains piled one on the other; and the fact that groups of closely related objects appear in widely scattered areas without apparent contact.

The number of known archaeological sites in the eastern states is exceedingly large, and there must be many more as yet undiscovered. From them has been taken an enormous mass of specimens in an extraordinary range of shapes. Fired clay pottery was found everywhere except in certain of the oldest sites. Stone work of many kinds and varying degrees of quality was even more widespread than pottery. Copper is represented by thousands of tools, weapons and orna-

Fig. 18. Area inhabited by the ancient Sculptors of the East.

Fig. 19. A sheet copper ornament representing a man with a feather headdress. 10½″ long, 6¾″ wide. From the Spiro Mound, Le Flore County, Oklahoma. Lent by the Ohio State Museum. (139/1-A)

ments. Of woodwork and textiles there is little trace because of the dampness of the climate, but we know from the accounts of early explorers that both were produced in quantity. Pearls from fresh-water mussels are rather surprising finds in many graves.

Little trace remains of architecture in the sense of actual houses or temples. But the earth mounds, which are the most spectacular feature of eastern archaeology, still stand as evidence of the Indians' skill in large-scale construction. Some idea of their achievement may be gained from the dimensions of the largest of all mounds, the Cahokia near St. Louis. It is 1080 feet long, 710 feet wide and about 100 feet high, covering an area of about sixteen acres.

Because of the existence of thousands of mounds of every shape and size, the term *Moundbuilder* has long been applied to the prehistoric eastern tribes. This custom has resulted in the belief that all mounds were the work of one mysterious, now vanished race which preceded the coming of the Indians. This belief is entirely wrong, for careful excavations have shown that the mounds were built by many tribes, some of them certainly the ancestors of Indian groups now living. Certain mounds are known to have been built after the coming of Europeans because of the presence in or under them of iron, glass and other things of European manufacture.

There are several main types of mounds. Flat-topped ones were built as foundations for temples and the dwellings of tribal leaders and officials. Those of conical shape served as burial places. Low ones, often of great breadth and length, are called effigy mounds because they are made in the shape of various living creatures. It is a strange fact that the makers of these mounds could never have had as clear a picture of their work as we have, since some of them, like the Great Serpent Mound in Ohio (Fig. 22), appear clearest in aerial photography. These mounds were used for burials but seem also to have had some connections with the social and religious organizations of the tribes. In addition there are numerous works of stone and earth made apparently for defense in intertribal warfare.

Fig. 20. A fragment of an engraved conch shell. About 6″ long. Spiro Mound, Le Flore County, Oklahoma. Lent by the University of Oklahoma, Norman.

The custom of building platform mounds seems to have been due to Mexican influences introduced only a few centuries before the coming of Europeans. It spread in a seemingly hit-or-miss fashion, sometimes appearing everywhere in a given area and sometimes only sporadically. In other words, it was a foreign custom taken up in varying degrees by different tribes with already established ways of life and cannot be considered a basic element of the great prehistoric eastern cultures.

All over the East, as everywhere else in America, can be found the crude artifacts of a modest level of technical and artistic accomplishments discussed on page 50. In addition to these primitive remains, there have been found in many sections very distinguished works of art of a purely regional character (Fig. 21). Finally, there appear scattered throughout the Mississippi drainage and the Southeast evidences of a high artistic development which shows undeniable Mexican influence (Fig. 20). This question of Mexican influence is one of

Fig. 21. A stone pipe. A spoonbill duck seated on a fish. 4½″ long, 2″ high. Hopewell Mound, Ross County, Ohio. Lent by the Field Museum of Natural History, Chicago. (56750)

the most puzzling in American archaeology. No objects actually made in Mexico have been discovered in the United States. But some pieces found in eastern sites are so similar in style and subject matter that the presence of Mexican Indians in this country has been suggested.

Archaeologists have divided prehistoric Indian life in the East into a number of cultures which have been named either for excavated sites, such as Hopewell and Adena, or after geographical areas such as Middle Mississippi. The difficulty in discovering the historical and regional relationship of these cultures is due to the fact that their manifestations rarely appear in segregated areas or at the same relative depth in sites.

Since only a few Indian groups remain in the area once occupied by the Sculptors of the East, it may be wondered what became of them. In the South many tribes died out, leaving no living descendants. Others were moved to Oklahoma in the early nineteenth century and are known today as the Five Civilized Tribes. The Iroquois of New York and some of the New England tribes are still in their former homes. Most of the tribes in the Ohio and Mississippi Valleys have disappeared or are represented by a few survivors living on reservations in Oklahoma or the

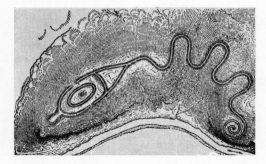

Fig. 22. Great Serpent Mound in southern Ohio. 1300′ long (following the curve), 2½′ to 3′ high. After Fowke.

Middle West. There are indications that some of these tribes are descendants of prehistoric groups, but details and proofs of such relationships are few.

The vanished life of the prehistoric southeastern tribes was quite unlike anything known among Indians today or in recent years. It had an exotic flavor not often associated with Indian culture in the United States. Around the great mounds clustered villages of perishable huts made of poles and

Fig. 23. The wife of a Timucua chief on her way to a ceremony. An engraving by de Bry of a drawing made in Florida by Le Moyne de Morgues in 1565.

grass or bark. The semitropical climate made more solid dwellings unnecessary and kept clothing for ordinary use at a minimum.

The Indians had a graceful and courtly manner which delighted the first explorers, the Spaniard, de Soto, and his companions. Something of its spirit was caught in the diary of Rodrigo Ranjel, de Soto's secretary. On May 3, 1540, he wrote:

". . . . then came the lady of that land whom Indians of rank bore on their shoulders with much respect in a litter with delicate white linen . . . . She was a young girl of fine bearing and she took off a string of pearls she wore on her neck and put it on the Governor to show her favor . . . ."

Stone Tools, New England. Left to right: grooved axe, 6″ by 4″; gouge, 13″ long; slate spear point, 10¼″ long; slate spear point, 5½″ long; slate spear point, 16″ long. Stone tools lent by Phillips Academy, Andover, Massachusetts; axe lent by the Peabody Museum, Harvard University, Cambridge. (Left to right: 72002, 50625, 52391, 58064, 62299)

These tools, except for the axe, are the work of the earliest Indian inhabitants of New England of whom remains have been found. These people specialized in the making of slate tools ground with almost mechanical precision. They resemble Eskimo tools, though no actual racial relationship is implied by the resemblance. The axe was a common tool of the late Algonquin tribes.

Left to right: grooved axe from Queen's County, New Brunswick, Canada; gouge from grave 163, Blue Hill cemetery, Maine, excavated by E. O. Sugden in 1913; slate spear point from grave 163, Blue Hill cemetery, Maine, excavated by E. O. Sugden in 1913; slate spear point from Stevens cemetery, Warren, Maine, excavated by W. E. Moorehead in 1915; slate spear point from Overlook cemetery, George's Valley, Maine, excavated by Gerard Towle in 1929.

Prehistoric Art: The Sculptors of the East   **63**

Iroquois Pot from Cayuga County, New York. 5½″ high, 5⅛″ in diameter. Lent by the Museum of the American Indian, Heye Foundation, New York. (6659)

Iroquois pottery became extinct about 1700 when it was finally superseded by brass or copper kettles introduced by European traders. Most Iroquois pots have heavy rim collars, many of which are square. On these collars appear the incised straight line designs so characteristic of the ware and of prehistoric northeastern Indian art in general. Some of the vessels, like the one illustrated here, have very simple human faces on the rims.

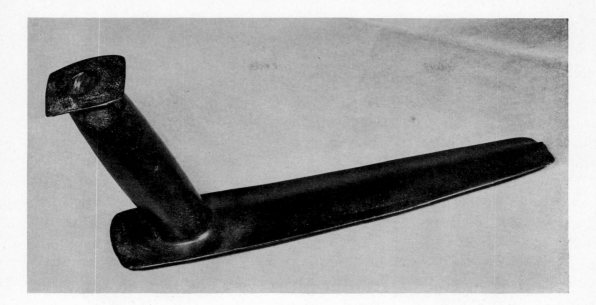

Stone Pipe from Virginia. 6⅞″ high, 15¼″ long. Lent by the Museum of the American Indian, Heye Foundation, New York. (18/2785)

The eastern tribes were pre-eminently the pipe smokers among prehistoric Indians, and as such they created a large number of pipe types. One of these has a flat oblong base on which is set a round bowl. Because such pipes resemble the famous Civil War battleship, they are called monitors. Though most monitor pipes are rather small, a few were made in large sizes. Of these large forms perhaps the most striking are those of the variety illustrated here. These have very tall bowls set at varying angles near the end of unusually long bases, some of which have flaring sides.

The finest of these big stone pipes have been found in or near Virginia, a region rather remote from the main centers of development in the East. Most of them are made of soapstone, chlorite, or serpentine, which are soft enough to carve easily and take a high polish. They are remarkably light in weight and usually dark green in color. Excavated in 1917 from a grave in Pulaski County.

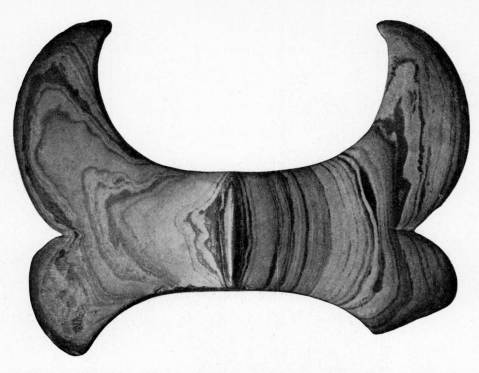

Banner Stone from Kankakee County, Illinois. 6″ across the wings. Lent by the Museum of the American Indian, Heye Foundation, New York. (13/9478)

Banner stone is the name given to a very large class of objects which have wing-like projections of many forms flanking a central section pierced vertically by an opening, usually round. The wings of most examples are much thinner than the centers. They are made from many kinds of stone, frequently beautiful in color or grain. Banner stones are found east of a line running from central Texas to Minnesota but are most common in an area including the Great Lakes and the states just south of them.

In its simplest form the banner stone seems to have been developed at a very early period in the interior of the Southeast. There is evidence suggesting that these small early types were weights placed on the shafts of dart throwers to give added momentum. There are also larger and less ancient types which are clearly too heavy for this purpose. Their size, elaborate form and beautiful finish suggest that they were symbols of authority, personal ornaments or religious paraphernalia which had evolved from the original utilitarian device. Though one of its tips has been broken, the banded slate example illustrated here gives an excellent idea of the symmetry and perfection of workmanship found in these abstract forms. The methods of making them and other types of the polished stone objects found so widely in the East are discussed on the opposite page. Collected before 1924.

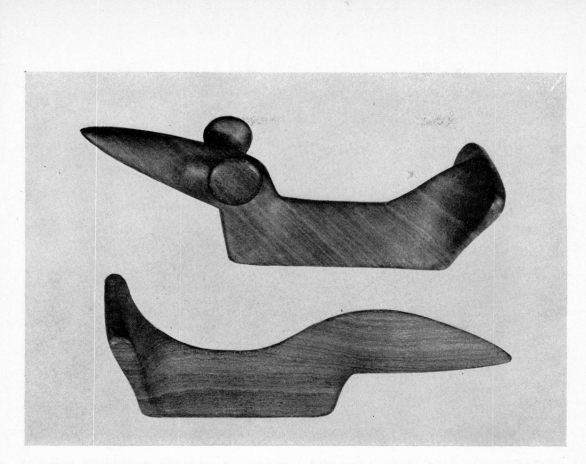

Bird Stones of grey banded slate from Illinois. Upper, Union County, 6⅜" long, collected before 1936; lower, Lawrence County, 5⅞" long, collected before 1938. Lent by the Museum of the American Indian, Heye Foundation, New York. (Upper, 18/9455; lower, 19/8022)

The eastern Indians' gift for sculpture is shown to no better advantage than by the simple abstract forms of their many polished stone tools, ornaments and various artifacts of unknown purpose. In this latter group are the figurines of the type illustrated here. Their purpose is an unsolved problem but their shape suggested the name bird stone.

Bird stones are found in a belt extending from the middle Mississippi Valley northeast into Canada and are the work of very early prehistoric inhabitants of the region.

All polished stone objects were made by pecking or chipping a piece of stone into a rough approximation of the final shape and then working out the details and finish with some natural abrasive like fine sandstone. Many of these polished artifacts were pierced with holes. Partially finished specimens show that in most cases drilling was done while the blocks were in the rough, in order to avoid breakage. The most perfect holes were made by placing sand on the spot to be pierced and rotating a solid stick or hollow cane on it. The sand did the cutting, the stick or cane merely providing the motive force. Copper or chipped stone drills were also used.

Prehistoric Art: The Sculptors of the East　　　　　　　　　　　　　　　**67**

Stone Pipe from the Tremper Mound, Ohio. 3⅞″ long, 2 9/16″ high. Lent by the Ohio State Museum, Columbus. (125-17)

Pipes in the form of realistically carved birds and animals are the best-known artistic products of the Hopewell culture in Ohio. This culture, named for the owner of a site in that state, is one of the most widespread in the eastern United States. Products of the culture have been found at sites in Ohio, several states around the Great Lakes, Louisiana and Florida. Artistically it is most developed in southern Ohio.

The Hopewell stone, copper and mica artifacts reproduced on these pages are outstanding examples of a high regional development that shows no stylistic influence from Mexico.

One feature of the culture was the building of mounds covering burial vaults in which many native treasures were deposited with the cremated bones of the dead. Small compartments in two mounds have yielded practically all of the Hopewell effigy pipes in existence. One, at Mound City, was excavated by Squier and Davis in 1846. About two hundred pipes were found and later sold in England. Sixty-nine years later another cache of pipes was discovered in the Tremper Mound. These are now in the Ohio State Museum. Details about the pipes are given on the opposite page. Excavated in 1915 by H. C. Shetrone. The bird represented is a hawk.

Stone Pipe from the Tremper Mound, Ohio. 2″ high, 3⅞″ long. Lent by the Ohio State Museum, Columbus. (125-24)

This pipe, representing an otter, is one of many found in the Tremper Mound discussed on the opposite page. One hundred and forty-five pipes were discovered in one small chamber inside the mound. Ninety of the bowls in the Tremper cache are effigies of birds and animals.

They are carved from greyish-tan Ohio pipestone, a very hard, dense clay technically described as a hydrated aluminum silicate. It is related to the better-known red pipestone, or catlinite, used for pipes by the Plains Indians. The carving was done with flint tools. The smoker held the pipe by one end of the base. The bowl is in the back or head of the animal and the mouthpiece is in the other end of the base. Large mouthpieces were not inconvenient for Indians since they did not place pipestems between the teeth as we do, but only between the lips. Excavated in 1915 by H. C. Shetrone.

Prehistoric Art: The Sculptors of the East **69**

Mica Ornament, Hopewell Mounds, Ohio. 9½″ long. Lent by the Ohio State Museum, Columbus

Thin mica sheets, cut in many shapes, have been excavated from the graves of important leaders of the Hopewell people. They appear to have been clothing ornaments. The mica came from mines in Virginia and North Carolina and was spread by trade through much of the Moundbuilder area. The hand is an important element in Southeastern prehistoric art. Excavated from the Hopewell mound group by H. C. Shetrone.

70   *Prehistoric Art: The Sculptors of the East*

From *Indian Arts in North America* by George C. Vaillant, Harper and Brothers, N. Y.

Copper Ornament from Mound City, Ohio. 8″ high, 12″ long. Lent by the Ohio State Museum, Columbus. (260/125)

Sheet copper plaques have been found in many prehistoric sites in the Mississippi Valley and in the Southeast. The few which show elaborate workmanship, like that on the eagle illustrated here, appear to have been used ceremonially or as the body ornaments of prominent leaders. Men and other living creatures, feathers and abstract forms are the usual subjects. Such plaques are the highest achievement in metal work of the prehistoric Indians north of Mexico. Practically all metal work was in copper, though a few objects of silver, gold and meteoric iron have been found.

The copper came from the Lake Superior region in nuggets pure enough to permit working without smelting and refining. The nuggets were beaten into thin sheets on which pierced, engraved, and repoussé designs were applied by pressure with sharp-edged bone tools. Cutting was done by rubbing on sandstone slabs. Annealing was the only metallurgical process known.

The highest development of copperworking seems to have been reached just before the discovery of America. The art has been extinct since then. Excavated in 1919–20 by W. C. Mills.

Stone Pipe from the Adena Mound, Southern Ohio. 8″ high. Lent by the Ohio State Museum, Columbus. (1200/10)

This remarkable pipe, the finest known example of Moundbuilder sculpture, is pierced by a tube with the mouthpiece in the headdress and the pipe bowl between the feet. No stem was used with it. The pipe is made of Ohio pipestone, a kind of fine grained clay of stony hardness, and is yellow-grey in front and brick red behind. The mottling is due to the presence of iron in the stone. The carving was done with flint tools and afterwards smoothed and polished with some abrasive.

The figure strongly indicates by its physical type and costume details the Mexican influence which is found widely in the Moundbuilder area. The whole treatment of the sculpture problem is reminiscent of Mexican stone carvings. The Adena culture which produced it was one of the most important in the central Moundbuilder area. Excavated in 1901 by W. C. Mills.

Prehistoric Art: The Sculptors of the East

Stone Face from Gallatin County, Kentucky. 10″ high, 6″ wide. Lent by the Museum of the American Indian, Heye Foundation, New York. (6/397)

This carving is one of a very few mask-like objects which have been found in widely scattered places throughout the East. Their purpose is unknown, but they may have been connected with the widespread ritualistic use of wood masks long common among eastern tribes. This mask was plowed up in 1860. The stone was originally white but has darkened to a brownish tan.

Prehistoric Art: The Sculptors of the East

Stone Pipe, Coffee County, Tennessee. 6″ long, 3″ high, 2″ wide. Lent by the Museum of the American Indian, Heye Foundation, New York. (7757)

Many large, heavy stone pipes carved in the effigies of men, birds and animals have been found in the states south of the Ohio River. A few were discovered in the Spiro Mound in Oklahoma.

These effigies are the largest of all Indian pipes, sometimes reaching a length of eighteen inches, a height of ten inches and a weight of eighteen pounds. They are much too large to be held while being smoked and must have rested on the ground when in use. The stem appears to have been a long, slender cane. The weight and size of these carved pipes are further emphasized by their broad sculptural treatment that is in sharp contrast to the miniature technique evident in the small Hopewell pipes illustrated on pages 68 and 69.

In his book *Antiquities of the Southern Indians*, C. C. Jones says: "As a general rule, the more remarkable of them may be regarded as the public property of the tribe: still, their presence in conical earth mounds containing but a single skeleton, would seem to indicate that some of them were the private property of noted personages, perhaps chiefs and medicine men. It is scarcely probable that the public peace-pipe would have been liable to inhumation." Collected by Joseph Jones near Manchester.

Stone Pipe from Ross County, Ohio. 3⅝″ high, 10⅝″ long. Lent by the Ohio State Museum, Columbus. (757-20)

This soapstone pipe represents a wolf. It is unique in that it shows the entire body of the animal instead of its head alone. Wolf effigy pipes are very rare and come almost exclusively from the Ohio Valley.

Large effigy pipes portray several types of subjects. Bird pipes are more common than those representing animals. Ducks, owls, hawks and eagles are the species usually carved, though doves, swans and various unidentified birds are not unknown. Of the animals, wolves, bears, dogs and members of the cat family are represented. There are many pipes in human form and some combine human and animal details.

The pipes form two major classes as far as basic shape is concerned. In the first, best illustrated in this book on page 85, the pipes are rather massive; and in the second, they are long tubes like the wolf pipe above. There are, of course, intermediate stages, of which the pipe on the opposite page is an example. In most cases the back of the effigy faces the smoker.

Considerable information about manufacturing stone pipes has been gained from specimens in every stage of completion. The general process was to peck the rough block into an approximation of the final shape and then finish the details by grinding. Some of the softer stones may have been carved with flint tools. The drilling methods have been discussed on page 67.

The Indians smoked ten or twelve species of tobacco, native to the country, and with few exceptions cultivated by the tribes. Other substances were frequently mixed with tobacco. Sumac leaves, red willow bark and the leaves of bearberry and manzanita are among the most common of these substitutes. The various mixtures are usually known today by the name kinnikinick.

Pottery Effigy Jar from Tennessee. 8½" high, 8" long. Lent by the Peabody Museum, Harvard University, Cambridge. (13998)

This effigy of a curly-tailed dog is a reminder that dogs were the only animals domesticated by the prehistoric Indians. Rather similar pottery dogs were made by the ancient Tarascan Indians of Mexico, and dog designs of various kinds appear in the arts of other ancient American peoples.

Effigy vessels of many kinds are especially common in the stone graves of Tennessee. The graves are lined and covered with slabs of stone and are often arranged in regular order in large cemeteries. This vessel was excavated in 1878 by Edward Curtiss.

Pottery Effigy Jar from Arkansas. 7½″ high, 10½″ long. Lent by the Museum of the American Indian, Heye Foundation, New York. (5/6528)

Many pottery vessels found in the eastern half of the Mississippi drainage are in the forms of various living creatures. The adaptation of these forms is extremely varied. In some cases the vessel is a conventional bowl or jar ornamented with the limbs and head of an animal. In other cases, as illustrated here, the entire jar is shaped like an animal body.

Frogs, fish, birds and animals native to the region were favorite subjects, but fantastic monsters combining features of various animals were also frequently used. Collected at Blytheville, Arkansas.

Prehistoric Art: The Sculptors of the East   77

Pottery Jar from Crittenden County, Arkansas. 8¾″ high, 7″ wide. Lent by the Museum of the American Indian, Heye Foundation, New York. (17/4149)

Jars modeled in the form of hunchbacks are quite common in prehistoric sites of the general Arkansas-Tennessee region, and in Mexico and Central America. Though their technique is relatively crude, they illustrate the Indian's accuracy of observation by their clear representation of the typical hunchback physique in all its details. Excavated in 1910–11 by C. B. Moore at the Rhodes Place.

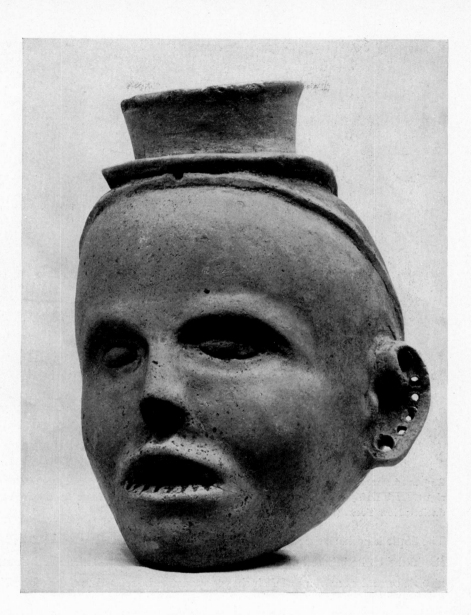

Pottery Jar from the Fortune Mound, Arkansas. 7″ high, 7″ in diameter. Lent by the Peabody Museum, Harvard University, Cambridge. (21542)

Buff-colored pottery jars representing human heads are characteristic products of the Arkansas-Tennessee region. In realism of modeling they range from crude images to the sensitive portrayal illustrated here. Their purpose and technique of manufacture are not known, though they appear to have been connected with burial rites. The custom of piercing the ears for a number of earrings survived well into the nineteenth century. Excavated in 1880 by Edward Curtiss.

Prehistoric Art: The Sculptors of the East

Engraved Pottery Bottles, Caddoan Type, Southwest Arkansas. Left, from Miller County, 7″ high; right, from Lafayette County, 6″ high. Lent by the Museum of the American Indian, Heye Foundation, New York. (Left, 17/4658; right, 17/4701)

The bottle is perhaps the most distinctive shape in southeastern pottery, since it is found nowhere else in the United States. Bottles are, however, common in Mexican and Central American prehistoric ceramics and some of their shapes appear to be related to those of the United States.

Bottles are found in great profusion in the Arkansas-Louisiana region. They may be decorated by painting, by incising in the damp clay before firing, or by engraving the hard surface after firing. The engraved designs are often accentuated by rubbing colored earth into them. The bottles shown here are polished black.

The making of engraved, tall-necked bottles lasted among the Caddoan tribes of southeast Arkansas until the seventeenth and eighteenth centuries. Such a late survival of purely pre-Columbian designs in the Southeast is remarkable. For there, more quickly than elsewhere, native arts disappeared after European conquest. Collected in 1911–12 by C. B. Moore.

Shell Mask, Tennessee. 8⅝″ high, 6⁷⁄₁₆″ wide. Lent by the Peabody Museum, Harvard University, Cambridge. (2238)

Mask-like objects cut from the asymmetrical sides of large, white ocean shells have been found in a number of southeastern states. Their position in graves near skulls or on the chests of skeletons suggests that they were either masks or pendants, but their use as masks for the dead seems more probable because the holes show no signs of wear from supporting strings. Excavated in 1869 by E. O. Dunning from the Brakebill Mound.

Prehistoric Art: The Sculptors of the East   **81**

Shell Gorget, Sumner County, Tennessee. 3⅞″ in diameter. Lent by the Museum of the American Indian, Heye Foundation, New York. (15/853)

Engraved white shell disks were worn by various prehistoric southeastern peoples as pendants, and many have been discovered on the chests of buried skeletons.

Mexican influence is very evident on this gorget. It is particularly apparent in the resemblance between the profiles on this gorget and those drawn in ancient Mexican manuscripts. Excavated in 1890 by W. E. Myer from the Castalian Springs Mound.

Shell Gorget, Sumner County, Tennessee. 3⅜″ in diameter. Lent by the Museum of the American Indian, Heye Foundation, New York. (15/855)

Designs engraved on the shell gorgets, or breast ornaments, of Tennessee and neighboring states are limited to certain subjects. These are the scrolled squares set with heads of ivory-billed woodpeckers illustrated here, other birds, spiders, rattlesnakes, scalloped circles, human faces and figures of a very Mexican character.

Both sexes wore these white ornaments, possibly as symbols of religious or civil authority. Each gorget was cut from the curved side of a marine conch shell and either engraved or pierced with openwork designs. The engravings are usually on the concave surface. Only stone tools were used. Excavated in 1890 by W. E. Myer from the Castalian Springs Mound.

Prehistoric Art: The Sculptors of the East   **83**

Stone Image, Wilson County, Tennessee. 17½″ high. Lent by the University of Tennessee, Knoxville. (1/1Wil)

This large sandstone figure far exceeds the few dozen others in existence in realistic indication of anatomical detail. The face is painted red and black. Stylistically the figure is related to the stone human figure pipes from the Spiro Mound. Stone images are found only in an oval area about five hundred miles long, of which western Tennessee is the center. They are usually buried in pairs, male and female, in stone boxes. Plowed up by a farmer near Lebanon in November, 1940.

Prehistoric Art: The Sculptors of the East

Stone Pipe from the Spiro Mound, Oklahoma. 8″ high. Lent by the University of Oklahoma, Norman. (B99-2)

The Spiro mound was excavated about ten years ago and yielded one of the largest and most spectacular collections yet discovered. Among the objects found were five very large stone pipes, one of which is illustrated here. Spiro was on the frontier between the Moundbuilders and the wild tribes of the West. Like some of the objects found in the mound, the pipes have a massive, barbaric strength. They show a strange style which may reflect a struggle between a tendency toward naturalistic portrayal and a tradition which demands conventionalization. Excavated in 1936 by Forrest Clements. The material is red bauxite.

Prehistoric Art: The Sculptors of the East

Wooden Mask from the Spiro Mound, Oklahoma. 11⅝″ high, 6¼″ wide. Lent by the Museum of the American Indian, Heye Foundation, New York. (18/9306)

Many prehistoric eastern tribes were in rather close contact or were connected by trade routes, so that ideas spread widely and assumed various forms. Antler headdresses are a case in point, for they appear in several techniques in widely separated areas. This wooden mask is from Oklahoma. In southern Ohio a copper helmet with antlers has been found. Georgia's Etowah Mound yielded an engraved shell ornament (page 91) showing an antlered man. Found in 1935.

Prehistoric Art: The Sculptors of the East

From *Indian Arts in North America* by George C. Vaillant. Harper & Brothers, N. Y.

Stone Disk from Mississippi. 8½″ in diameter, 1″ thick. Lent by the Ohio State Museum, Columbus. (14/23)

About a dozen large flat disks, some with engravings on one face, have been found in the Mississippi Valley and the Southeast. They are believed to be palettes on which paint was ground because traces of red and white paint have actually been found on some of them. Most of them have notched or scalloped rims.

The shallow engravings on these disks show skulls, hands, eyes and rattlesnakes, all common subjects in prehistoric eastern design. The disk illustrated here is decorated with two intertwined rattlesnakes with feathered heads which suggest Quetzalcoatl, the Plumed Serpent of Mexico.

Found in 1870 in a mound in Issaquena County. The material is brown sandstone.

Prehistoric Art: The Sculptors of the East

Limestone Bowl, Moundville, Alabama. 13¾″ long, 9″ wide, 4″ deep. Lent by the Museum of the American Indian, Heye Foundation, New York. (17/20)

Stone bowls have been rather uncommon in southeastern archaeological excavations. The lack of metal carving tools and the ease with which pottery could be made are possible reasons for the scarcity of stone vessels. Their rarity and elaborate decoration may indicate that they were reserved for ceremonial use.

The bottom of the bowl is covered with a pattern of plumage carefully executed in low relief. On it appear the legs and feet of the bird folded to follow the curve of the bowl. The species of bird represented on this bowl has not been identified.

The Moundville group is one of the most important in the South. Its mounds have yielded great numbers of artifacts which show a high artistic development with strong suggestions of Mexican influence. Excavated in 1905–06 by Clarence B. Moore.

Prehistoric Art: The Sculptors of the East

Stone Image from the Etowah Mounds, Georgia. 25″ high, about 45 lbs. in weight. Lent by Phillips Academy, Andover, Massachusetts. (82/R113)

Stone images of dead chiefs and their wives were placed in the now vanished temples of certain southeastern tribes. Very few of these images exist today. These simple yet imposing figures are good examples of the monumental quality found in so much Indian sculpture. Found in 1925 by W. K. Moorehead on Mound C, carefully buried in a stone box.

Prehistoric Art: The Sculptors of the East

Monolithic Axe from the Etowah Mounds, Georgia. 15″ long. Lent by Phillips Academy, Andover, Massachusetts. (61466)

Axes with stone or copper blades and wooden handles were made in many places on this continent. Replicas of these axes made from one single stone block are sometimes found in the West Indies, Central America and the southeastern United States. Since these monolithic tools are too brittle to serve any useful purpose and show exceptionally painstaking care in workmanship, it seems certain that they had some ceremonial function.

Excavated in 1926 by W. K. Moorehead on Mound C. The material is polished blue limestone.

Prehistoric Art: The Sculptors of the East

Shell Gorget from the Etowah Mounds, Georgia. 2½″ in diameter. Lent by Phillips Academy, Andover, Massachusetts. (82/R115)

Circular white shell ornaments similar to those from Tennessee (pages 82 and 83) appear in many prehistoric southeastern sites. All were worn on the chest suspended from a cord passing around the neck and were cut with stone tools from the walls of conch shells found in the Gulf of Mexico.

The significance of the designs cannot be explained with certainty. But the gorget on this page may illustrate a Creek Indian myth of two warring groups, one led by the eagle and the other by a long-tailed bird. The eagle won the battle and cut off his enemy's head. On the gorget can be seen the eagle man, with wings and antlers, holding in one hand the head of his rival.

This figure with wings and antlers closely resembles those from the central Mississippi drainage which represent the mythical Horned and Feathered Serpent. This creature is in turn strongly reminiscent of Mexico's Plumed Serpent. Excavated in 1928 by W. K. Moorehead from Mound C.

Prehistoric Art: The Sculptors of the East **91**

Pottery Bottles, Caddoan Type, North Central Louisiana. Left, 7⅝″ high; right, 5¾″ high. Lent by the Museum of the American Indian, Heye Foundation, New York. (Left, 17/3682; right, 17/3248)

The bottles illustrated here are exceptionally fine examples of two of many varieties. That on the right, though unusual in shape, shows the scroll style at its best in an allover pattern executed with great skill and taste. In contrast, the bottle on the left depends on beauty of shape for its appeal. Both are polished black. That on the left has red paint rubbed into the incised lines.

These bottles belong in that group of southeastern wares which are probably, from the artistic standpoint, the finest in the region. They were made in the lower Mississippi Valley in the seventeenth and eighteenth centuries. Technically this is in the historic period after the arrival of Europeans; but culturally the pottery is prehistoric, being purely an outgrowth from the aboriginal past. As is frequently the case in Indian art, very few of thousands of the pottery vessels found in the area attain a great degree of perfection, but those that do are very superior.

These vessels in their lack of paint and use of carved curving designs are typically eastern as opposed to southwestern wares with their painted angular patterns. Northeastern and central wares are unpainted and ornamented with combinations of straight lines. The Pacific coast north of San Diego produces no pottery. Excavated in 1908–09 by C. B. Moore.

Pottery Bottle, Caddoan Type, North Central Louisiana. 6″ high, 6″ in diameter. Lent by the Museum of the American Indian, Heye Foundation, New York. (17/3711)

Short-necked globular bottles, common to this region, exemplify the southeastern Indian potters' ability to create well-rounded shapes, unaided by the potter's wheel.

The design illustrated is one of that variety of the widespread southeastern scroll style developed by the Caddoan peoples around 1700 A.D. Work of this quality is very rare. The design is incised, or drawn in the damp surface before firing. Excavated in 1908–09 by C. B. Moore at the Glendora Place, Ouachita County. The color is dark brown.

Prehistoric Art: The Sculptors of the East

Pottery Jar, Ossabaw Island, Georgia. 16½″ high. Lent by the Museum of the American Indian, Heye Foundation, New York. (17/4486)

Jars of this kind when dug from mounds usually contain skeletons. The jars were themselves "killed" by punching a hole in them to release their spirit, a widespread Indian custom.

Allover stamped designs are most fully developed in Georgia. The patterns were pressed into the soft, unfired vessels with wooden blocks on which designs in low relief had been cut. The designs may be plain checkers or, as here, variants of the southeastern scroll style. Excavated in 1896 by C. B. Moore in Mound A, Ossabaw Island, Bryan County.

Wooden Alligator Head, Key Marco, Southeastern Florida. 10¼″ long. Lent by the University of Pennsylvania Museum, Philadelphia. (40718)

This alligator head and the deer head following are among the finest examples of a school of wood-carving which flourished in southern Florida during the fifteenth century. The origin of these carvings may be safely ascribed to the now extinct Calusa Indians. Besides the works illustrated, there have been found a number of other masks, figures in the round and utensils of varying nature. All were dug from deposits of wet muck and many of them, on drying, shrunk greatly or broke beyond repair. Fortunately some of the finest pieces were made of a wood which withstood the strain of drying.

Many carvings of the school are marked by a sensitive realism which is not found elsewhere in wood sculpture north of Mexico. Northwest Coast wood-carving, with its highly developed stylization and formal exaggeration, is entirely unrelated; and the extremely simplified conventionalizations of southwestern wooden figures are equally so. The rather slightly developed wood-carving of the eastern tribes does lean toward realism but achieves it less fully than did that of the Florida sculptors.

It has been suggested that there may be some relationship between the art of our Southeast and that of the West Indies and northern South America. But careful examination of the evidence has so far given little backing to the idea. Excavated in 1895 by F. H. Cushing.

Prehistoric Art: The Sculptors of the East   **95**

Wooden Maskette, Key Marco, Southeastern Florida. 10¾″ long overall. Lent by the University of Pennsylvania Museum, Philadelphia. (40707)

The deer, alligator, wolf and other masks excavated at Key Marco were found in circumstances which suggest they were made for ceremonial use. All retain traces of paint, which had been used to emphasize the sculptural forms. Parts of some of them, like the deer's ears, had leather hinges so that they could be moved with strings. The eyes had shell inlays to increase the lifelike effect.

In delicacy of treatment and degree of realism this deer head is unequalled in Indian art and is the finest surviving creation of the fifteenth century Calusa wood-carving discussed at more length on the previous page. Excavated in 1895 by F. H. Cushing.

The Painters of the Southwest

Fig. 24. Area inhabited by the ancient Painters of the Southwest.

The area called the Southwest has been variously defined; in this book it is considered to include Arizona and New Mexico with adjoining portions of Colorado, Utah, California, Nevada and Mexico. The high north and east section is an elevated plateau broken by canyons and forest-covered mountains. At a much lower altitude lies the southwestern part, a rather level plain with some isolated groups of low, sharply cut mountains. Though often called desert country, the Southwest is by no means a vast expanse of sand like the Sahara. On the contrary, more or less sparse vegetation and many kinds of rocks and soils are everywhere present. The climate is dry and hot, though winters on the plateau may be rather cold.

Indians have lived in this region for a very long period. Chipped stone points of the Folsom type, first found in New Mexico, date back about fifteen thousand years on geologic evidence. For at least two thousand years the Southwest has been occupied by peoples who still live there. For them there has been no break between past and present, so that the line between prehistory and history, archaeology and ethnology is very difficult to determine.

Compared with the Southeast and its little understood tangle of cultures, the Southwest presents a quite clear picture of ancient peoples in two well-established major cultural groups, each of which has subdivisions

Fig. 25. A Basketmaker burden basket made 500-600 A.D. Canyon del Muerto, Arizona. The designs are red and black. 15″ high, 32″ in diameter. Lent by the University of Colorado Museum, Boulder. (2558)

Fig. 26. Cliff Palace, largest of the ruins in Mesa Verde National Park, southwestern Colorado. It was abandoned about 1300 A.D. after about two hundred and fifty years of occupancy.

with individual characteristics. In addition there are certain indications of other cultures which are not as yet fully understood. Each group has always lived in approximately the same section and followed the same way of life. Naturally there has been considerable intermingling between them and some movement of peoples. But the essential place and pattern of each culture is clear.

The best-known group is that of the town-dwelling Pueblos and their forerunners, the Basketmakers. These tribes, formerly called Basketmaker-Pueblo, are now frequently given the name Anasazi, the Navaho word for ancient people. They lived in the northern and eastern parts of the Southwest, with some extensions toward the south. The Basketmakers, so called because baskets were their chief product, appear in dated history about the beginning of the Christian era as a scattered race of hunting and wild-seed-gathering people. Agriculture and pottery do not appear in the early phases of their development. From this simple beginning there evolved the complex Pueblo civilization with its great terraced stone and adobe apartment houses, highly developed arts and crafts, and elaborate social and religious systems. This civilization reached its height in the fourteenth and fifteenth centuries, and is still the basis for modern Pueblo Indian life.

Fig. 27. A black-and-gray pottery jar from Mesa Verde National Park, southwestern Colorado. 8″ high, 15½″ in diameter. It was made in the thirteenth century. Lent by the Mesa Verde National Park Museum, Mesa Verde, Colorado.

On the low-lying desert of southern Arizona lived the Hohokam tribes. The name is the modern Pima word for ancient people. Their place in dated history is not so clearly marked as that of the Anasazi, but is roughly contemporaneous with that group. They were farmers on the flat desert river valleys and nourished their crops with great irrigation systems. Their villages were small communities of separate houses made of interlaced poles and brush plastered with adobe mud. The Hohokam were prolific makers of a buff or tan pottery with red designs executed with a freedom far removed from the rather stiff Pueblo fashion. Weaving and carving in stone and shell were done also, but in general their arts and social systems were less developed than among the Anasazi. The Hohokam may be the ancestors of the present day Pima and Papago.

Of the other less clearly defined cultures, the most important is the Mogollon of southwestern New Mexico. The culture is linked to both Hohokam and Pueblo but has certain definite characteristics of its own, such as polished brown pottery with red designs.

All these cultures utilized the same raw materials and techniques, though in varying degrees. Because of its resistance to decay, pottery in a considerable range of shapes decorated with a bewildering number of painted designs has come down to us in larger quantities than anything else. Carving in stone and shell was well developed by the southern groups and not entirely neglected by the northerners. The latter were especially skillful in the use of turquoise. Cotton textiles also appear to have been most developed by the Pueblo group. Basketry, the greatest craft of the early Anasazi, declined somewhat in importance after the invention of pottery between 300 and 400 A.D. With a few exceptions woodwork was rudimentary. The Anasazi group is noteworthy for its achievements in architecture. The many-storied Pueblo buildings are the greatest

Prehistoric Art: The Painters of the Southwest

Fig. 28. A black and white cotton bag woven in a damask technique. 12½″ long, 5¾″ wide. Fourteenth century A.D. Found in a ruin near Montezuma Castle, Arizona. Lent by the Montezuma Castle National Museum. (123)

expressions of this art north of Mexico. A typical pueblo is pictured on page 120.

All these crafts gave the tribes of the Southwest an opportunity to use two-dimensional painted decorations. Their art reaches its climax in murals, pottery decorations, weaving, and mosaic executed in turquoise and stone. Their masterly treatment of flat spaces suggested the name, The Painters of the Southwest, used in this book.

Southwestern archaeology is unique in that many of its phases can be accurately dated. This remarkable state of affairs is due to the tree ring calendar worked out by Dr. A. E. Douglass.

The calendar is based on the fact that trees add a layer to their girth every year. When the tree is cut these layers appear as rings on the stump. Rainfall controls the width of each ring, wet years producing wide rings and dry years narrow ones, so that each tree is a record of the rainfall during its life. Though the ring pattern of each tree reflects purely local climatic conditions, some of the major details of ring pattern will appear in all trees over a large area in which the rainfall is about the same everywhere, as it is in the Southwest. To construct a tree ring calendar, a modern tree is cut down and its ring pattern transcribed on paper in a series of lines of uneven length, a line to each year. Then a log or beam from some early historic building is cut and its ring pattern is transcribed. Since both sets of rings will show a few of the same major details, the older near its edge and the younger near its center, the two records can be fitted together so that the calendar stretches back from the last outer ring on the modern tree to the first inner ring on the old beam. Then the ring record of a beam in a still older building or ruin is fitted on that of the first beam, extending the calendar still further back in time.

By thus fitting together the records from many beams, it has been possible to extend the calendar back to 11 A.D. Any ruin in which wood is found can be dated by comparing the ring pattern of the wood with the master chart which reaches from 11 A.D. to 1940. Ruins which have no wood in them are dated by cross dating, that is, by comparing the objects found in them with those from ruins dated by the tree ring calendar.

Pottery Jar, Hohokam, from Southern Arizona. 18″ high, 21¾″ in diameter. Lent by Gila Pueblo, Globe, Arizona. (44772)

The Hohokam culture was developed by a people quite distinct from the better-known Pueblo tribes. It dates back about two thousand years and survives today, in some details at least, among the Pima and the Papago. Most Hohokam pottery is buff with red decorations made with an iron oxide paint. Like those of the Pueblos, the vessel walls were built up with strips or rolls of clay. But they were finished by striking them on the outside with a wooden paddle against a stone held inside; this is called the paddle-and-anvil technique and was not known to the Pueblos.

The jar illustrated here is typical of the Sacaton Red-on-buff ware made around 1000 A.D. The extreme development of the shoulder and the details of the design are especially characteristic of the period. Excavated in 1935 at Snaketown.

Prehistoric Art: The Painters of the Southwest

Pottery Bowl, Hohokam, Southern Arizona. 10¾″ in diameter. Lent by Gila Pueblo, Globe, Arizona. (43855)

Hohokam pottery is occasionally decorated with amusing painted figures of men and animals. These little drawings are executed with a broad, free-flowing line quite unlike the rather stiff draughtsmanship of the Pueblo painters.

The figures are often repeated in long rows. Despite their simplicity, they throw much light on the human activities and wild life of the time and region.

The bowl illustrated here is Santa Cruz Red-and-buff ware and was made about 800 A.D. Further details about Hohokam pottery are given on the previous page. Excavated in 1935 at Snaketown.

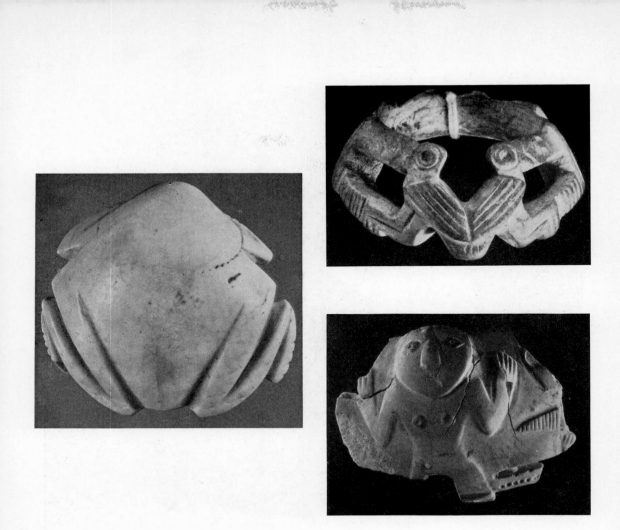

Shell Ornaments, Hohokam, Southern Arizona. Upper right, finger ring ⅜″ high, 15/16″ in diameter; lower right, fragment 2¼″ long, 1¾″ wide. Lent by the Los Angeles Museum, Los Angeles. (145 and 142). Left, pendant 2″ long, 2″ wide. Lent by the Brooklyn Museum, Brooklyn. (4618)

The Hohokam were the greatest users of shells in the prehistoric Southwest. The shells were all obtained by trade with tribes on the Pacific coast or the Gulf of California. Thousands of pieces of shell work have been found in Hohokam sites. But because they were used as funeral offerings in the cremation rites of the people, relatively few undamaged pieces have been found.

The finest pieces of shell work are bracelets and finger rings made of *Glycymeris* shells, and pendants of *Pecten*, *Turritella* and *Cerithium* shells. The best rings and bracelets are carved in relief with frog, snake and bird patterns. The same creatures are represented in the pendants.

The ring and fragment were excavated in 1930 by Arthur Woodward from the Grewe site. The pendant was collected in 1903 by Stewart Culin at Flagstaff, Arizona.

Prehistoric Art: The Painters of the Southwest

Pottery Bowl, Mimbres Culture, New Mexico. 10⅝" in diameter. Lent by the Taylor Museum, Colorado Springs. (10/59)

Deep food bowls decorated with highly conventionalized living creatures are the most characteristic products of the Mimbres potters. Like all artists of the ancient Southwest, the Mimbres were also masters of geometric designs arranged in complex patterns, but their interest in organic forms is unique in that region. Painting of this type was done over only a relatively short period. It shows such outstanding imagination and is so consistent in its style that one cannot but wonder if this school is not due to the influence of one singularly gifted individual.

The origins of the Mimbres school of painting have probably evolved as a whole from a mingling of the art styles of the three cultures described on pages 98 and 99. Twelfth century A.D. Excavated in 1925 by C. B. Cosgrove at the Swarts Ruin.

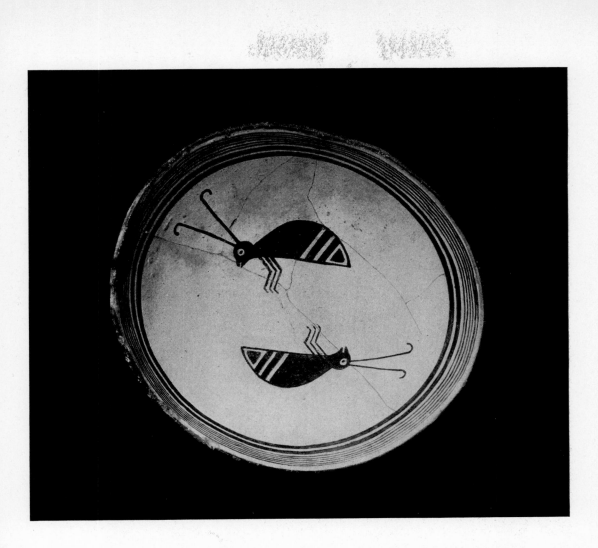

Pottery Bowl, Mimbres Culture, New Mexico. 9″ in diameter. Lent by the Peabody Museum, Harvard University, Cambridge. (94548)

The food bowls on these two pages give some idea of the so-called naturalistic school of painting on twelfth century Mimbres black and white pottery. In the work of this school the subjects range from insects and animals through human beings to strange and delightful monsters of unknown identity.

Even if he built them from geometric form elements, the Mimbres artist always gave his living subjects a strange animation of their own, and succeeded in bringing out their most essential characteristics. Mimbres painting is also outstanding for the skill of its technical execution. The warping, due to faulty firing, is characteristic of the ware. Excavated in 1925 by C. B. Cosgrove at the Swarts Ruin.

Prehistoric Art: The Painters of the Southwest   **105**

Woven Sandals, Basketmaker, Northeastern Arizona. 9″ long, 3″ to 4″ wide. Lent by the University of Colorado, Boulder.

Sandal weaving with fine yucca fiber cord was a great craft of the Basketmakers of thirteen hundred years ago. Though the soles of such sandals were easily worn out, they were often woven in most intricate patterns and decorated in black and red. This elaboration of perishable material reveals the Indians' feeling for fine craftsmanship. Found in 1924 by E. H. Morris.

Pottery Jar, Pueblo Culture, New Mexico. 15″ high, 15″ in diameter. Lent by the Laboratory of Anthropology, Santa Fé, New Mexico. (I.A.F. 1456)

In the years around 1000 to 1200 A.D. the Indians living in the Rio Grande drainage south of Albuquerque were influenced in their art by either trade wares or actual visitors from Chaco Canyon, a center of Pueblo culture in northwestern New Mexico. One result of this influence was the appearance of the ware called Socorro Black-on-white, of which the jar illustrated here is a fine example. At the time the jar was made, the geometric black and white design style of the ancient Pueblos was in what might be called its classic phase, when its patterns, derived from the basketry of some fifteen hundred years ago, had been completely transformed to fit painting on pottery. Found about 1930 near Grants, New Mexico, by a shepherd.

Prehistoric Art: The Painters of the Southwest   **107**

Pottery Bowl from East Central Arizona. 10″ in diameter. Lent by Earl H. Morris, Boulder, Colorado.

Shallow bowls for food and general household use have long been made by the Pueblo Indians. The wide-mouthed shape illustrated here is that generally found in the drainage of the Little Colorado River in Arizona. Pueblo pottery types changed frequently and often rapidly in design and form. These changes can be traced by excavations in the layers of village rubbish piles, and dated by the tree ring calendar explained on page 100. Each pottery type has been given a name derived from its location and color scheme. The type illustrated here is known as Four-mile Polychrome and was made about 1375 A.D. Its colors are black and white on red.

Prehistoric Art: The Painters of the Southwest

Pottery Bowl, Pueblo, Northeastern Arizona. 12″ in diameter. Lent by the Peabody Museum, Harvard University, Cambridge. (76226)

In the general region occupied today by the Hopi Indians there developed, through several centuries after 1200 A.D., a number of yellow to orange pottery types. For ceramic quality and beauty of design the best of these are often considered to be the finest products of southwestern Indian potters. Their patterns are frequently conventionalizations, in several colors, of bird forms.

In 1896 the celebrated Nampeyo, one of the few great Indian artists known by name, based her revival of fine pottery making among the Hopi on a study of these wares. Excavated in 1900 by Frank Russell, at Ruin 4, Kokopnyama.

Prehistoric Art: The Painters of the Southwest   **109**

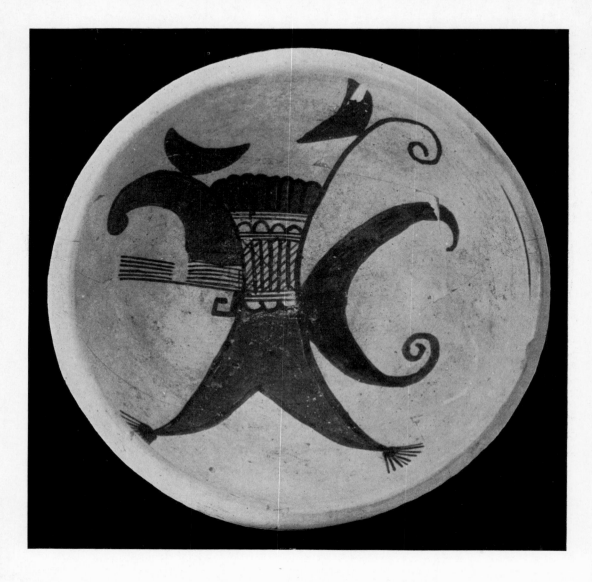

Pottery Bowl, Pueblo, Arizona. 12″ in diameter. Lent by the Peabody Museum, Harvard University, Cambridge. (37.111.10/12537)

This bowl was excavated at Awatovi, the ruined village where the murals illustrated on the next two pages were found. The ware is Jeddito Black-on-yellow.

The decoration is an excellent example of the subtle method of balancing an asymmetric design through careful arrangement of a wide range of form elements. This type of composition is most frequently found among the Hopi and their predecessors. Excavated in 1937 by J. O. Brew at Awatovi.

110   *Prehistoric Art: The Painters of the Southwest*

Mural Painting from Kawaika-a, Northeastern Arizona.   7′ high, 6′ wide.   Lent by the Peabody Museum, Harvard University, Cambridge.

This reproduction of a mural from a ruin represents a falling warrior pierced by an arrow.

Southwestern mural painting is an ancient art first practiced on smooth canyon walls. When adobe plaster began to be used as a wall finish a thousand years ago, the Pueblo painters found in it an ideal background for their work and have continued to use it ever since.

Most prehistoric murals have disappeared. But enough traces remain to give some idea of the art and its distribution. Large numbers of paintings have been found—at Kuaua near Albuquerque, New Mexico, and in the Awatovi group of ruins in northeastern Arizona. The murals were painted over a long period of years on successive layers of plaster placed on the walls of kivas, or ceremonial chambers. Further details about them are given on the next page. Excavated in 1939 by J. O. Brew.

Prehistoric Art: The Painters of the Southwest   **111**

Mural Painting from Awatovi, Northeastern Arizona. 7′ high, 11′ wide. Lent by the Peabody Museum, Harvard University, Cambridge.

The reproductions of prehistoric Pueblo mural paintings in this book and exhibit were made on adobe plaster panels by modern Hopi painters working from scale drawings prepared by Watson Smith and Penrose Davis of the Peabody Museum.

The mural illustrated here is one of three running in a continuous band around the walls of a kiva or underground ceremonial room. It was painted in the first half of the sixteenth century, at the very close of the prehistoric period, and is therefore purely Indian in character and details. Some of these details are extremely interesting because of the light they throw on the continuity of Pueblo culture. An example is the mask on the central figure. It is essentially the same as that worn by the modern Hopi kachina dancer called Wuwuyomo. The belt worn by the central figure is exactly like those used today and the kilts and sashes on the smaller figures are of the same type as modern ones. Above all, the style of the whole picture—and of the others in the series—is like that of modern Hopi Indian painting.

The Awatovi murals were executed on successive coats of plaster, so that to study the whole series it was necessary to peel these layers off one by one. This was done by glueing cloth to the outermost layer, pulling off both cloth and layer, mounting the painting on a prepared backing and unglueing the cloth with a solvent. Excavated in 1938 by J. O. Brew.

Pictographs

Native races all over the world have made designs and pictures on the surfaces of boulders and cliffs. The pictures are made by painting, drawing, scratching, pecking or grinding, or by combinations of these methods. No rock pictures were made north of Mexico by carving with a chisel or other sharp-bladed tool. Rock pictures are customarily called pictographs, though the term *petroglyph* is sometimes given to those made by processes other than painting and drawing.

Fig. 29. Boulder covered with petroglyphs, Ambrose, North Dakota.

Rock pictures are found all over the United States and Canada, though more commonly in the West, and have been made since the earliest times. They are still made today in certain sections. In the Southwest, for example, modern Navaho drawings in charcoal may be found on top of ancient Pueblo rock paintings.

Pictographs show a very wide range in design style. Some are entirely abstract, some have highly conventionalized natural forms, and others are remarkably realistic. Occasionally combinations of all three styles may be found. The arrangement of design elements is usually more or less haphazard. Some pictographs, however, are well composed. In size they range from small to gigantic.

Fig. 30. Pictograph from a cave near Santa Barbara, California.

The designs cannot all be classified by type, though there are a few distinct local styles like the strong abstract designs of southern California (Fig. 30), the large human figures of Utah (Fig. 31), the animal drawings of the prehistoric Pueblos and the simple massive figures of the Northwest. The best-preserved painted pictures are those on canyon walls in the almost rainless Southwest. Here are found immense galleries of paintings and carvings, one of which, from Barrier Canyon, Utah, has been reproduced full size for this exhibit.

The many attempts to read meanings in pictographs have met with little success. Some of the more realistic ones show clear pictures of various human activities, but the significance which most pictographs may have had has been lost to us. All except modern ones are too old to come within the knowledge of living Indians. It is usually impossible to date rock pictures, though they obviously were made over a long period of time.

Despite these enigmatic qualities, pictographs are important in the study of Indians. The fact that related designs appear in different localities offers suggestions about intertribal relations, and from the more realistic pictures one can learn details of clothing and customs.

Fig. 31. Basketmaker pictograph from southern Utah.

Living Traditions

In the prehistoric section, incomplete knowledge of cultural background made it preferable to divide this book according to information about art styles and techniques gained from the actual specimens. In the section devoted to Living Traditions, however, where we are familiar with the life and ways of the people, it seems advisable to establish divisions on a broader basis. To determine this basis it is necessary to consider the whole bewildering complex of Indian life and to decide which way of dividing it is best in this case.

The variety of languages, ways of living, art forms and even physical types found among the native inhabitants of the United States and Alaska is very great. There are over two hundred tribes in existence that speak dozens of languages, show wide diversity of physical types and create as great a variety of art forms as can be found on any continent.

Offhand it would seem most natural to divide the Indians of the United States and Alaska into units that either show the same physical characteristics or are made up of people speaking related languages, since such divisions would stress common ancestries. A closer study of the living tribes reveals, however, that either racial or linguistic inheritances alone are often quite unrelated to the cultural development of a people. For example, among the tribes who speak languages belonging to the Uto-Aztecan language stock we find not only hunting nomads like the Comanche, who are warlike and aggressive and have developed a social system with a distinct emphasis on individualism, but also the Hopi, who are peaceful agriculturalists living in settled villages and believing in collective activities. These two groups are unquestionably related through both blood and language, but hundreds of years of living in different surroundings, following different occupations, have made their life more similar to that of unrelated neighbors who use the same type of resources than to that of a related tribe living in an entirely different environment.

Since the arts of a tribe reflect its mode of life more clearly than they do its linguistic and racial inheritance, it seems most suitable here to overlook boundaries of language and ancestry and to divide the section of Living Traditions into eight culture areas, each containing groups of Indians who have closely related ways of living. These eight groups, whose locations are shown on the map in Figure 32, are:

THE PUEBLO CORNPLANTERS   THE SEED GATHERERS OF THE FAR WEST

THE NAVAHO SHEPHERDS   THE HUNTERS OF THE PLAINS

THE APACHE MOUNTAIN PEOPLE   THE WOODSMEN OF THE EAST

THE DESERT DWELLERS OF THE SOUTHWEST   THE FISHERMEN OF THE NORTHWEST COAST

To these groups has been added a ninth, the Eskimo Hunters of the Arctic. The Eskimo is only

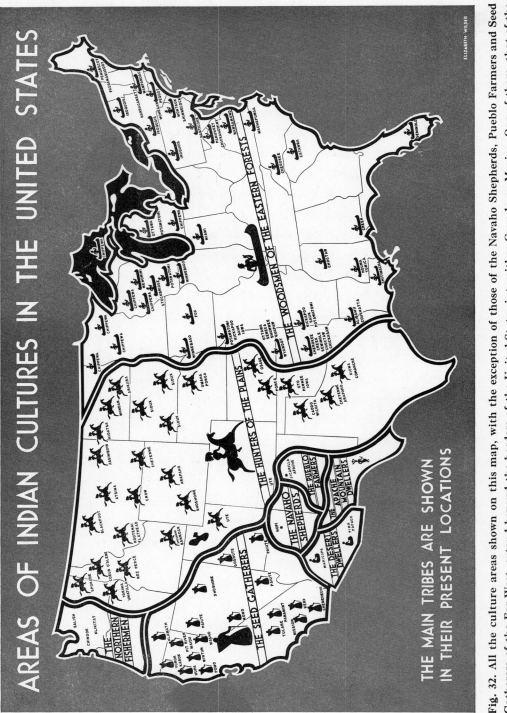

AREAS OF INDIAN CULTURES IN THE UNITED STATES

THE MAIN TRIBES ARE SHOWN
IN THEIR PRESENT LOCATIONS

ELIZABETH WILDER

Fig. 32. All the culture areas shown on this map, with the exception of those of the Navaho Shepherds, Pueblo Farmers and Seed Gatherers of the Far West, extend beyond the borders of the United States into either Canada or Mexico. One of them, that of the Northern Fishermen, stretches across the entire coast of British Columbia into Alaska where it joins the area of the Eskimo Hunters of the Arctic.

remotely related to the Indian, but his mode of living is an excellent example of a native American culture based on the ingenious use of the resources available in his section of this continent. One group, the Woodsmen of the North, has not been given a chapter here, because most of its members live in Canada and, in any case, the variety of its crafts is relatively small.

The occupations implied in the names of these various groups are still followed in some cases, although in others they are being rapidly replaced by new ones brought in by the white man. Fishing, for example, is still the main occupation of the Fishermen of the Northwest Coast, while the Hunters of the Plains have had to abandon the chase since the white man spoiled their land for hunting and destroyed the game.

The fact that cattle raising and agriculture have been recently introduced in the Plains area as a substitute for the old hunting life will undoubtedly affect the culture of its tribes in the future. But since these new occupations were not of their own choice and are still essentially foreign to many of them, their social and religious life and their art are still based on the roving life of the nomad.

One culture area, that of the Navaho Shepherds, is named after an occupation that was not native to this country. Sheep and the knowledge of their care were brought to the Navaho country by the Spaniards, but the Navaho has adjusted his life so perfectly to a shepherd's existence that today he is as true a sheepherder as the Pueblo is a farmer.

Thus we see that the names used here for the various culture areas do not necessarily indicate that the groups still follow the occupation implied in the name. Neither do they indicate that the occupation has been followed by a group's ancestors since time immemorial. The names given to the various areas simply refer to those circumstances that have conditioned the contemporary culture of each group.

In using the map of the areas of Indian culture in the United States, it should be realized that the divisions in real life are never so clear-cut as they appear on paper. On the border between two areas there always live people who have adopted some characteristics of both their neighbors. In eastern Washington, for example, among the groups living between the Hunters of the Plains and the Fishermen of the Northwest Coast, buckskin work of the Plains type is done as well as Northwest Coast basketry. Sometimes it even happens that a characteristic of one culture is found transplanted to a group living deep in the adjoining area.

The important arts of the historic period and their distribution are briefly as follows:

Painting in some form is found everywhere. It is at its best on southwestern pottery, on Northwest Coast woodwork and on skin articles from the Plains. Painting in other sections of the country, though less fully developed, is used for many purposes. The modern school of Indian water-color painting is discussed in a later chapter.

The finest and almost only true sculpture is that of the Northwest Coast. This school of sculpture is one of the high spots in Indian art. There were and still are secondary centers producing simpler work in the Southwest, on the Plains and around the Great Lakes.

Pottery making has been actively carried on in the Southwest without a break for sixteen hundred years. The great pottery art of the eastern tribes, with a few very small exceptions, did not long survive the impact of white civilization and became extinct about two hundred years ago. But for the first centuries of the historic period it was, in some sections, at its best.

Metalwork has had several centers. In the eighteenth century the Iroquois of New York and thereabouts were the leading makers of silver jewelry. From them, in the early nineteenth century, the center of development passed to the Mississippi Valley and Great Lakes tribes. Many tribes used German silver as well as silver. This Middle Western school of metalwork is still flourishing in Oklahoma. The finest silver jewelry is that of the Navaho and Pueblos of the Southwest. Since its beginnings about 1850 this art has expanded remarkably and achieved great fame.

Basketry in one form or another exists from coast to coast. It has been made in the greatest variety and with the most skill in the West. California is the main center of the art, with the Southwest ranking second and the Northwest Coast third. East of the Rocky Mountains there is a considerable development of basketry in the South and to a lesser extent in the Northeast. Neither, however, compares in quantity and quality with western work.

Weaving has had four centers of development. Of these the Southwest is by far the most important. There weaving on the true loom has had a continuous history among the Pueblos since about 800 A.D., and among the Navaho, most prolific of Indian weavers, since about 1700. Of the three other centers, one is around the Great Lakes and produces flat, rectangular wool bags on a simple weaving frame. An equally simple device is used by the Tlinkit weavers of southeastern Alaska, makers of the colorful, intricately patterned Chilkat textiles. The fourth weaving center was in the general region of Puget Sound, Washington. From it came coarse blankets woven on a roller loom with dog and mountain goat wool. Certain Middle Western and southeastern tribes have been skilled in the very complex braiding of broad sashes. These same tribes formerly used buffalo wool to weave bags, belts and garters, and today make much woven beadwork.

Embroidery with porcupine quills or with commercial glass beads has always been a craft of the northern United States, a few small regions excepted. The areas from the Great Lakes to New England and from the central Plains north into Canada are its important centers. Quillwork is done on skin or birch bark, and beadwork on skin or cloth. Appliqué embroidery is, in design, an outgrowth of the older birch bark engraving and quillwork. It is done with colored silk ribbons which are cut into figures and sewn to cloth or skin garments. This work had its beginnings in the eighteenth century and is found today in Oklahoma and around the Great Lakes.

The Pueblo Cornplanters

The home of the Indian tribes known by the general name Pueblo lies today in northern Arizona and New Mexico. Formerly their range extended south into Mexico and throughout much of Utah and Nevada as well as southwestern Colorado. The country is one of vast distances. For the most part it is a high plateau, rather dry but crossed here and there by fertile river valleys. High, pine-covered mountains rise in a number of ranges. Flat-topped mesas dominate the landscape and have played an important part in the human history of the region. Outcroppings of colored sandstone and shale are another feature characteristic of the country.

Fig. 33. Area inhabited by the Pueblo Cornplanters.

The Pueblo area of today stretches in a crescent from northeastern Arizona to north central New Mexico. To the west are the villages of the Hopi. Some still occupy their ancient sites atop high mesas; others, of recent origin, are on the valley floors near the bases of the mesa cliffs. One of these villages, Oraibi, was founded over a thousand years ago and is the oldest continuously inhabited town in America. Near the center of the crescent, south of Gallup, New Mexico, lies Zuni, the only remaining member of the group of villages once famed as the Seven Cities of Cibola. Still farther east in the general neighborhood of Albuquerque are the towns of the Keres. At the eastern end of the crescent are the villages of the Tanoan people, scattered along the Rio Grande Valley from Isleta, near Albuquerque, north to Taos. Another town of the Tanoan group, Jemez, lies isolated on the Jemez River northwest of Albuquerque. The total Pueblo population is about sixteen thousand.

For centuries there have lived in this area groups of Indians who, although their languages differ, are united by their common dependence on agriculture. The growing of corn, which began about 500 A.D., was especially important and influenced every aspect of their lives. The other two important field crops, beans and squash, appeared even later. Beans were especially important because they provided an abundant supply of proteins which was largely responsible for the rapid growth of the Pueblo civilization in the eleventh to fourteenth centuries. Proteins had hitherto been obtainable only in small amounts in meats.

Pueblo, the Spanish word for village, is the common name of these Indians. It was given them by the Spanish because the Indians lived in permanent villages of stone or mud brick houses. The existence of these villages is due entirely to the Indians' activity as farmers, for farmers must

Fig. 34. Taos Pueblo, a village of the Tiwa Indians, north of Santa Fé, New Mexico.

stay near their fields to care for them and must have places in which to store their harvests. Out of these needs, through a process of evolution, grew the typical Pueblo architecture (Fig. 34).

When the ancestors of the Pueblos began to grow corn they built shallow pits in which to store their scanty crops while they lived as wandering hunters. As their crops became more plentiful, they built increasingly large underground storerooms. Eventually, when so much corn was produced that it was no longer necessary to seek food elsewhere, the people settled down in villages of houses patterned after their storage pits but larger. They then built stone corn cribs on the surface. The final step in the development of their architecture came when they concluded that stone buildings on the surface were better than sunken pit houses. Once this step had been taken the building of very large, many-roomed masonry homes followed.

Soon after corn came to them from Mexico, about fourteen hundred years ago, the Pueblos found that farmers must adjust their lives to the ceaseless rotation of the seasons, coordinating their social, governmental and religious systems with the cycle of nature. Centuries of this systematic life in closed communities have developed in the Pueblo world a sense of order, a smoothly functioning collective society and a conservative ritual with elaborate paraphernalia (Fig. 35). The security they gained from their strong permanent homes and their stored-up crops gave them leisure during the winter months to invent and perfect the greatest variety of crafts found among Indians.

Their life as farmers made these people fully aware of the plant and mineral resources of their homeland. Cotton for weaving and many plants for basket making were familiar to them, as were the location and quality of various clays for the making of pottery. The oldest of their crafts, basketry, is woman's work and in its most highly developed forms is unequalled in the beauty and variety of its color (Fig. 36). The women have also been expert potters for fifteen centuries, molding the clays of the land into many graceful shapes and painting the smooth surfaces with numerous intricate designs.

Pueblo pottery design styles have had a long and interesting history. It begins with the designs on the baskets and plant fiber textiles of the Basketmakers, the predecessors of the Pueblos. About 400 A.D., when pottery was either invented locally or introduced from elsewhere, there arose the problem of decorating it. After experimenting with various designs, the women reverted to those on baskets, which they already knew well, and began to adapt them to pottery painting. As the Pueblo civilization evolved, this new art progressed and eventually became one of the most im-

Fig. 35. Hopi painted wood batons carried in the Mamzrau ceremony. 24¾″ long, 5¾″ wide. Lent by the Peabody Museum, Harvard University, Cambridge. (3574 and 3575)

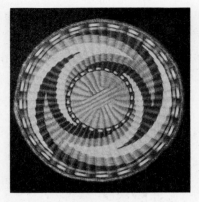

Fig. 36. Hopi basket tray. 13″ in diameter. Denver Art Museum, Denver. (YH3-P)

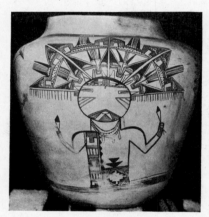

Fig. 37. Hopi pottery jar. 15¾″ high, 14½″ in diameter. U. S. Office of Indian Affairs, Washington, D. C.

Fig. 38. Jemez cotton shirt with wool embroidery. 23″ long. Denver Art Museum. (RJ-3-P)

portant in the whole area. A number of different design styles were evolved. Fashions in patterns rose and fell, died out and were revived, influenced each other and were affected by the work of the non-Pueblo tribes. The early Spanish period brought first confusion and then decline to the arts of the Pueblo world. At its end, about 1700, most of the area had been abandoned and many of the major regional pottery designs had become extinct. But in the few villages that survived the Spanish conquest, of which all but a few exist today, purely local styles came into being and from them have evolved the patterns made today (Fig. 37).

Since about 800 A.D. Pueblo men have been creating the most elaborate types of woven cloth made by any Indian group, first using native cotton, and later wool, which was introduced by the Spanish. The beauty of this fine cloth was further enhanced by painting, brocading and, above all, embroidery (Fig. 38). Men have also long been the makers of shell, stone and turquoise jewelry, and of stone and shell figurines inlaid with turquoise. As painters and carvers the men created in wood, skin and featherwork the colorful paraphernalia of their complex dances and secret ceremonies.

Protected by its conservative institutions, the steady rhythm of this ancient life still beats. Early recognition that the proximity of the white man meant danger to their own spiritual life resulted in the tribal organization of the Pueblos soon after the coming of the Spaniards. The office of governor, introduced by the invaders, was incorporated by the Pueblos into their tribal government and became an effective shield against foreign influence; for the governor was able to protect the real spiritual leaders of the community from outside interference. The wisdom of the Pueblos, reflected in this move, enabled them to preserve their own cultural values better than any other Indian group and at the same time to live successfully, though surrounded by the aggressive civilization of the white man.

Living Traditions: The Pueblo Cornplanters

Pottery Drum Jar, Zuni Pueblo, New Mexico. 18½″ high, 21″ in diameter. Lent by the Taylor Museum, Colorado Springs.

The ordinary Indian drum is made of wood with a deerskin head. But at Zuni, and among the Navaho and Apache, pottery vessels are sometimes used. Zuni drum jars, usually white with black and red designs, are large and have out-curving rims made especially to hold the binding cord which keeps the skin head stretched tight. Large drums such as this one are beaten simultaneously by a number of men. The tone is less resonant than that of a wooden drum.

Indian musical instruments are very limited in the number of basic types, though each type has many varieties. Drums and rattles are the most frequently used since they are ideal for providing the rhythmic basis for singing, the chief form of music among Indians. There are also flutes, whistles and, among the Apache only, a crude fiddle suggested by our violin.

Zuni drum jars are notable for their finely proportioned and monumental shapes. The painted design is a deer, an animal much favored by Zuni potters. Collected about 1931 by Harry Garnett at Zuni.

Pottery Jar, Santa Clara Pueblo, New Mexico. 11″ high, 14½″ in diameter. Lent by the Laboratory of Anthropology, Santa Fé, New Mexico. (I.A.F. 311)

The most familiar modern Pueblo pottery is perhaps the polished black ware made in the villages of the Tewa tribe north of Santa Fé. The deep black color is not applied by painting, but by smoking in the following manner. Each batch of pottery is fired in a kiln, made of dried cakes of animal manure, which is destroyed in the process. To produce the black color the blazing mass is smothered with powdered fuel. The smoke, impregnated with carbon from the burnt fuel, cannot escape and envelopes the red-hot pottery on which it deposits an even black coating.

The shiny finish of this ware is not produced by glazing, but by rubbing with a smooth stone before firing. Glaze has not been used in any way on Pueblo pottery since about 1700. Prior to then it was used at several places and periods but only to make line decorations.

The jar illustrated here, a very typical Santa Clara form, was made about 1900.

Pottery Bowl, Santo Domingo Pueblo, New Mexico. 7¼″ high, 15¼″ in diameter. Lent anonymously.

Among the Pueblo Indians the painting of designs on pottery is done just before firing, the final step in pottery making. With one exception (a black made from the bee weed) the colors used are various minerals ground in water. The brush is a slender section of yucca leaf. It is chewed at one end to remove the pulp surrounding the fine fibers which are the "hairs" of the brush.

The designs are applied freehand. The main dividing lines of the pattern are drawn first and the details filled in afterward. No two designs are exactly alike, but each village uses its own basic design elements over and over again in slightly differing combinations. Pottery making is women's work, although in recent years the husbands of some women who produce a great deal of pottery have helped by doing the painting. The designs are usually without significance, though some of their elements may once have been symbolic.

The food mixing bowl illustrated here gives a good idea of the style most frequently used at Santo Domingo. The pottery design of this pueblo is the most rigidly abstract of all and seems to reflect the uncompromising conservatism of its makers. Twentieth century.

Living Traditions: The Pueblo Cornplanters

Embroidered Wool Dress, Acoma Pueblo, New Mexico. 50″ long, 46″ wide. Lent by the Taylor Museum, Colorado Springs. (20/924)

The Pueblo woman's dress has been for some hundreds of years an oblong piece of handwoven cloth worn wrapped around the body. The same type of cloth was also sometimes used as a shawl to cover the head and shoulders. It was made of white cotton till Spanish times, since then of black wool. Embroidery, one of the several ways of decorating these garments, reached its height in the black Acoma and Laguna dresses with their elaborate red, blue and green designs. Such shawls have not been made for many years and are now very rare. Most of the designs can be traced back to those found on southwestern basketry of twelve hundred or more years ago.

Pueblo embroidery appears to be pre-Spanish in origin, though the question is not definitely settled. Like weaving it is a man's art. Except among the Hopi it has declined greatly in recent years, but its revival in Indian Service schools gives good hope for future re-establishment. Made during the middle of the nineteenth century.

Kachina Dolls from Pueblos in Arizona and New Mexico. Left, Zuni mudhead clowns; center, Chaveyo, the Hopi cannibal Kachina; right, Hemucikwe from Zuni, representing the Earth and Sky. 10" to 16" high. Lent by Austin Ladd, Coolidge, New Mexico.

The term *kachina* is applied by the Pueblo Indians to several kinds of supernatural beings such as the spirits of the dead, cloud and rain spirits, and local spirits inhabiting springs. The exact number of these beings is unknown, but at least five hundred appear in the mythologies of the different villages. Every village, however, does not believe in, or even know about, all of these spirits.

Kachinas are believed to live in sacred places near the villages and to visit them on stated occasions. The belief is that the masked Indian dancers representing kachinas on such occasions are actually turned into supernatural beings by wearing masks. This faith in the power of masks is common among many native races throughout the world.

The kachina cult exists everywhere in the Pueblo region. It is strongest in the western part, among the Hopi and Zuni, decreases as one moves eastward to the Rio Grande villages and is very weak, or perhaps nonexistent, at Taos, the easternmost Pueblo.

The carved and painted cottonwood figures illustrated here are dolls made in the images of three of the masked dancers. These dolls are made by the men as playthings for the little girls. Collected before 1938 by Berton I. Staples.

Living Traditions: The Pueblo Cornplanters   **127**

Mask, Zuni Pueblo, New Mexico. 26″ long, 10″ high. Lent by the Brooklyn Museum, Brooklyn. (04.196)

This is the mask of Saiyatasha, one of the principal characters in the Shalako ceremony, the culmination of a year-long cycle of religious observances held at Zuni. During the Shalako, which occurs about December first, the gods come to Zuni to bless new houses. The man who impersonates Saiyatasha must be of great dignity and moral uprightness, for the character is much loved by the people. He must be willing to make many sacrifices and above all "his heart must be good."

In the following quotation from the *Forty-third Annual Report* of the Bureau of American Ethnology, Dr. Ruth Bunzel describes the mask:

"On his head he wears the downy feather and a bluejay feather 'because he is a priest,' and also the feathers of the summer birds. The feathers are actually fastened to a prayer stick. He has one long blue horn (whence his name, 'long horn'), on the right side, 'because he brings long life to all his people.' His eyes are long, too. But on the right side his eye is small. That is for the witch people, so that they may not live long, but on the left side his eye is long for the people of one heart, 'so that they may have long life.' Black goat's hair hangs from the horn, and over the forehead. White cotton threads hang down behind. The mask is made of elk skin. The face is painted turquoise. The collar is made of elk skin stuffed with wool." Collected in 1904 by Stewart Culin.

Dance Mask from Zuni Pueblo. 21⅜″ high, 14⅞″ wide. Lent by the Brooklyn Museum, Brooklyn. (14.0256)

This mask is one worn in a so-called mixed dance in which many kinds of masks appear. Some are traditional types but others, like that illustrated here, are the original creations of individuals. The thin wooden panel which rises above the face is customarily called a tablita, the Spanish word for a small board. Tablitas are worn by women dancers at many pueblos. Collected in 1903 by Stewart Culin at Zuni.

Living Traditions: The Pueblo Cornplanters

War Gods, Zuni Pueblo, New Mexico. 2′ and 2½′ high. Lent by the Brooklyn Museum, Brooklyn. (03.128 and 03.124)

The Zuni have two war gods of whom images are made for use in certain regularly recurring ceremonies of the pueblo. After the ceremonies are completed, the images are placed in shrines on nearby mountains. As new ones are made the old ones are removed and piled nearby. They are carved by special craftsmen from the wood of lightning-struck pine trees.

These figures are the product of an intensely conservative Indian group and are perhaps a modern survival of a very ancient sculptural style. Collected in 1903 by A. Vanderwagon.

Living Traditions: The Pueblo Cornplanters

The Navaho Shepherds

Sheep raising has been the foundation of Navaho life since about 1600, when the Spanish imported sheep in quantity into the Southwest. The home of the Navaho is well suited to sheep raising. It lies chiefly in northeastern Arizona but extends into New Mexico and Utah. It is a land of pine-clad mountains and plateaus, often cut deeply by rose-colored canyons and sloping out into broad valleys. Many isolated buttes tower above the valley floors and give a dramatic aspect to the landscape. Grasses, leafy plants and shrubs grow everywhere, though somewhat thinly because of the dry climate. Water for men and animals comes from a few flowing streams, mountain springs and pools of rain water in the red

Fig. 39. Area inhabited by the Navaho Shepherds.

Fig. 40. A Navaho man's blanket, displayed as worn. This type is usually called a "chief" blanket. Made about 1870. 72″ long, 54″ wide. Lent by the Denver Art Museum, Denver. (RNch-16-G)

sandstone which crops out in many places in the Navaho country.

The tribe today numbers approximately fifty thousand, the largest in the United States. Its increase since 1870 has been phenomenal and still continues. The women weave thousands of rugs on looms set up near their log and earth houses. The children tend the great herds of sheep, goats and horses. Many of the men are silversmiths. Food comes from the herds, from gardens and corn fields and from the traders' stores. The clothing of the Navaho, today made exclusively of commercial cloth, is a blend of Indian, Mexican, Civil War American and modern influences. Native clothing of blankets or skins passed out of use long ago.

The Navaho and the related Apache came to the Southwest about six hundred years ago from Canada and Alaska. They belong to the Athapaskan family, of which there are branches along the Pacific coast as well as in the North. All the Athapaskans have a faculty for absorbing new elements into their culture. Small when it arrived in the Southwest, the Navaho tribe increased rapidly by incorporating groups of other Indians, and formed much of its present culture by borrowing from the different peoples it encountered as time passed. From the Pueblos were

Fig. 41. A Navaho poncho with terraced figures. 82″ long, 53″ wide. Lent
by the Laboratory of Anthropology,
Santa Fé, New Mexico. (L10/367)

Fig. 42. A Navaho blanket with sharply
angled figures. 75″ long, 50″ wide. Lent
by Mrs. O. L. N. Foster, Denver. (15)

adopted various social and religious customs, the growing of corn and the arts of sand painting and weaving.
From the Spanish came the horse and sheep. The Mexicans were the source of silversmithing and many details
of dress; and today various material aspects of modern
American life are being widely adopted.

The tribe's most celebrated craft, weaving, was introduced about 1700 when Navaho and Pueblos were
thrown into close contact as a result of the Pueblo revolt
against the Spanish. The Navaho took over the spinning
method and loom developed by the Pueblos perhaps a
thousand years earlier, and learned how to card, or
comb, the tangled wool with tools adopted from the
Spanish. In the Pueblo world men were the weavers,
but among the Navaho they have been replaced by
women. The Indian gift for color and design shows nowhere to better advantage than in Navaho weaving.

The patterns used on Navaho cloth have undergone a
number of changes. At first the only designs were stripes
in a few dark colors similar to those still found on Pueblo
blankets. Striped blankets made up most of the weaver's
production till fairly recent times. About 1800 a new
style appeared. It retained some striping, but added
squares, diamonds and other simple figures with terraced
boundaries (Fig. 40, coarse terracing; Fig. 41, fine terracing). At about the same time the Indians acquired
English baize, a kind of flannel called bayeta in Spanish,
which they raveled to obtain fine threads dyed bright
red, a color hitherto unobtainable.

The new style and materials were responsible for the
best weaving ever done by the tribe, that made in the
middle of the nineteenth century. Trouble with the
Government and the captivity of the tribe at Fort Sumner, New Mexico, between 1863 and 1868, gave the
craft a severe setback. But it was soon revived, appearing

132

this time in a new guise. The early terraced figures were largely replaced by elaborate patterns with sharply zigzagging edges (Fig. 42). Aniline dyes and commercial yarn, introduced about 1875, extended the range of color and design.

Until this time the Navaho had been weaving only blankets. However, the large increase in white settlement and the development of commerce in Indian textiles resulted in a demand for floor rugs. Consequently about 1895 there appeared a new design style with borders, not used previously, and large patterns running lengthwise instead of across. The

Fig. 43. Navaho silver bracelet set with hand-cut New Mexican turquoise. Lent anonymously.

colors changed also, browns, grays, black and white replacing the brighter shades used before. This type of thick floor rug has been the most common Navaho woven product ever since. But about 1915 a revival of older styles and color schemes was begun. Today an increasing number of fine blankets and rugs are being made which display patterns based on the old terraced tradition of the fifties and sixties.

Silversmithing, another great Navaho art, was learned from the Mexicans about 1853. Jewelry, bridle ornaments and other small objects were wrought from coins and silver ingots previously

Fig. 44. Navaho silver necklace. The large beads are conventionalized pomegranates, a form adopted from the Mexicans. They are commonly though mistakenly called "squash blossoms." Lent by Hon. Harold L. Ickes, Washington, D. C.

hammered to the desired thickness, or cast from molten metal in soft sandstone molds. Though dependent upon Mexico for its technique, Navaho silversmithing uses forms derived from a variety of sources. The bridles, buttons and beads were adapted from Mexican work, but other forms and designs were borrowed from the Plains tribes, who in turn had received them from white jewelers in the eastern states. Rings, bracelets and belt plates were of this origin.

The crescent pendant, an old Mediterranean evil-eye charm, reached the tribe through both sources. A modification of this crescent is shown on the pendant of the necklace in Figure 44. The designs on Navaho silver are made with the same stamps or dies used on Mexican leatherwork. They are for decoration only and have no symbolic significance.

In the art of sand painting the Navaho are pre-eminent (Fig. 45). Sand paintings are designs created by sprinkling different colored powdered earths and rocks on a bed of sand spread on the floor. The pictures are representations of gods, spirits and sacred places in Navaho religion. They are executed freehand with extraordinary skill, are often highly complex in detail, and always well composed. They are made by medicine men as part of religious ceremonies for healing.

Weaving, silversmithing and sand painting are the best-known Navaho crafts, but pottery and baskets are also made, though not to their former extent. The plain cook pots of the Navaho are especially interesting, because they are related in form and manner of decoration to the pottery made by many far northern peoples of North America and Europe. It is possible that these pointed bottom pots are descended from those which the ancestors of the Navaho brought from Asia.

The most interesting thing revealed by a study of Navaho crafts is the tribe's ability to change adopted forms until they become their own. In this, as in other fields, these people have shown that, given the opportunity, they can combine their own ideas with ours to create a truly native civilization adapted to life in the modern world.

Fig. 45. A sand painting from the Shooting Chant. Four goddesses surrounded by a rainbow are shown. Lent by the Museum of Navajo Ceremonial Art, Santa Fé, New Mexico.

Living Traditions: The Navaho Shepherds

The Apache Mountain People

Apache is not the name of any single united tribe, but of a widely distributed group of Indians. Until the inroads of white civilization forced it into bitter warfare which ended in confinement on reservations, the Apache nation consisted of many bands loosely united by related dialects and customs, but functioning largely as independent units. Because they now live in the mountains of the Southwest, we refer to the Apache in this book as the Mountain People.

In central Arizona were various bands now called the Western Apache. Where Arizona, New Mexico and Mexico come together lived the Chiricahua. The Mescalero wandered over southern New Mexico, and the Jicarilla were in the northern part of that state. Long ago there were bands on the Plains—Lipans, Querechos, Cuartelejos and others—of which little is known but the names.

Fig. 46. Area inhabited by the Apache Mountain People.

The Apache are close relatives of the Navaho and, like them, came down from the North six or seven hundred years ago. Both belong to the Athapaskan family, one of the last to come from Asia. The Navaho, settling near the old established Pueblo villages, adopted many of the accomplishments of Pueblo civilization. But the Apache remained roaming hunters and raiders until their wars were over and even today are known for their look of untamed pride.

Fig. 47. A Western Apache basket. 27″ high, 22¾″ in diameter. Lent by the American Museum of Natural History, New York. (50.2/3363)

Apache territory was vast before reservation days. To the east it lay on the plains of Colorado and Texas, and its western end included most of Arizona and New Mexico. This barren land was a fitting home for the hardy virile people who wrested from it the essentials of life. Food came from game, desert plants, and corn grown in fertile pockets hidden in the hills. Huts were made of poles and grass, and garments were cut from animal skins. Tough-soled high boots were worn for protection against the stony, cactus-covered ground. The Apache, men and women alike, were great horse people, thoroughly at home in their apparently hopelessly inhospitable environment, and capable of great feats of endurance.

Fig. 48. Western Apache basket, made about 1910. 23″ in diameter. Lent by William Denman.

Despite their hard, savage life the Apache have been far from lacking in artistic and technical ability. In basket making, their major art, they produce large bold forms decorated with patterns of great inventiveness (Fig. 47). The designs on the large shallow basket bowls often give the impression of rapid whirling motion (Fig. 48). Apache medicine men, painting on skins, have created some of the most forceful of Indian painted designs (page 31). Pottery was too fragile for the nomadic life and was rarely made. Beadwork was done occasionally, but was never an important craft.

Their religion and rituals were simple, yet their "Devil Dance," with its fantastic masks and vigorous gestures, is one of the most dramatically exciting of all Indian ceremonies.

At present the Apache, some eighty-two hundred in number, are peaceful farmers and stockmen. Forced to abandon their own way of life, their successful adaptation to an alien culture is remarkable, and their economic rehabilitation after disastrous defeat has been outstanding.

The Desert Dwellers of the Southwest

Fig. 49. Area inhabited by the Desert Dwellers of the Southwest.

Across the flat sunbaked plains of southern Arizona flow two sluggish rivers, the Gila and the Salt, both tributaries of the Colorado. Around the edges of the plains and scattered over their surface craggy blue mountains rise in the shimmering heat. In spring curious desert plants display their brilliant flowers, while above them tower the weird sahuaro cactus trees. In this beautiful but seemingly uninhabitable waste live most of the Desert Dwellers, tribes who have learned how to secure a living from their harsh environment.

These desert tribes include three geographic groups which are alike in their ability to live in the desert but differ greatly in language and customs. One group in southeastern Arizona near Phoenix and Tucson includes the Pima and the Papago, closely related in language, and the Maricopa, who speak another tongue. The Pima and the Maricopa have old agricultural traditions, while the Papago depend to a greater extent on the resources of the desert. On the lower Colorado River, between the end of its great canyons and the Gulf of California, lives the second group, made up of the Yuma, the Mohave and the remnants of several related tribes. All speak languages of the Yuman family. The life of these people is closely tied to the river which irrigates their corn fields with its floods and provides them with fish. Linguistic cousins of these river people are three small tribes which are members of the third group—the Walapai and Havasupai, living on the high plateaus south of the Colorado River between Grand Canyon and Boulder Dam, and the Yavapai, inhabitants of the central Arizona mountains. These are rather primitive seed-gathering, basket-making tribes, though the Havasupai have corn fields in the bottom of Cataract Canyon, a tributary of the Grand Canyon, and live there part of the year.

Simplicity marks most phases of Indian life in this region. There is no elaborate social organization, for the tribes are split into little semi-independent bands or villages, each controlling its own affairs. Religious ceremonies are simple and the general picture of the Desert Dwellers' life is one of peaceful and unexciting industry.

For food most of them depend on their crops of corn, beans and squash, supplemented by the products of such desert plants as mescal, giant cactus, mesquite and the pinyon tree of the mountains. For meat they hunt rabbits, deer and other game. The Colorado River tribes are great fish

Fig. 51. A Pima basket bowl made in 1939. 14¾″ in diameter. Lent anonymously.

eaters, and rely on the seasonal floods to irrigate their fields. Irrigation is also practiced by the eastern group.

In the old days there was little clothing except a breechcloth for men and a short fiber skirt for women. Nowadays the people dress like whites. Among the southern groups the houses are flat-roofed or domed buildings of mud-plastered logs and poles; the Havasupai and their group use light structures of poles, grass and leaves.

The crafts of these tribes are closely associated with the desert. From its scanty vegetation they take much of the material used in basketry, such as the hooked black seed pods of the devil's claw and yucca leaves. Cattails and willow twigs they gather from the watercourses. Pima and Papago baskets are particularly important because of their masterly treatment of complex geometric designs (Figs. 51 and 52).

The pottery of the Pima, Papago and Maricopa is polished red, either plain or with black designs made with mesquite gum paint. The modern Maricopa, and to a lesser extent the Pima and Papago, make quantities of pottery for trade. Among the Yuma and Mohave, pottery is closely related in appearance to the prehistoric red-and-buff ware of the region. In addition to bowls and jars these tribes make dolls and many-spouted bottles (color plate page 25). All Desert Dweller pottery differs in technique and design styles from that of the Pueblo potters to the north.

Formerly the Pima group wove plain cloth from wild cotton. But the art is almost extinct today. The Papago carve massive wooden bowls and the Colorado River tribes make netted collars of blue and white beadwork.

The population of the three groups today is: Yuma-Mohave, seventeen hundred and fifty; Havasupai-Wala-pai-Yavapai, nine hundred and fifty; Pima-Papago-Maricopa, twelve thousand.

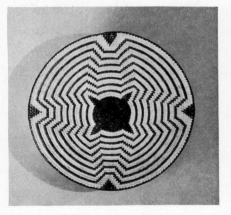

Fig. 52. A Papago basket made in 1940. 8¼″ in diameter. Lent anonymously.

Living Traditions: The Desert Dwellers of the Southwest

The Seed Gatherers of the Far West

The most striking fact about California and Nevada Indian life is the existence of a large number of little tribes, each with its own language and customs. The topography of the region is chiefly responsible for this condition. In California the Sierras and the coast ranges are cut up into many deep valleys, in almost every one of which lived some small tribe which, through centuries of virtual isolation, evolved a language and culture of its own. In the more open southern desert and in Nevada, isolated groups developed independently around widely separated water holes or springs.

The Indian tribes of California and Nevada are technically less advanced than their neighbors in the Southwest or the North. This is not due to a lack of innate ability but to a natural environment that did not demand or favor the development of complex civilizations. Everywhere in this region, even in the desert, a great variety of plant life provided the food of the Indians and also the raw materials for their greatest craft, basket making. Agriculture was unknown, for the people depended on wild crops for their vegetable foods—the acorn, pine nuts, many kinds of grass seeds, and the roots or bulbs of various plants. The rivers running into the sea provided fish for some of the northern tribes, and deer and rabbit meat supplemented the prevailing diet of vegetable food.

The daily life was largely devoted to the endless and difficult labor of gathering food, for living on natural crops is not just a matter of lying under trees and letting their fruits drop into one's hands. Going through the many steps of preparing the acorn for use and trudging miles over the hills while gathering seeds a handful at a time were wearying

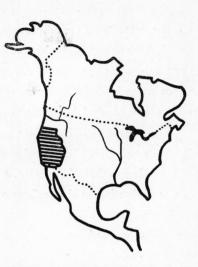

Fig. 53. Area inhabited by the Seed Gatherers of the Far West.

Fig. 54. A Karok effigy of albino deerskin trimmed with red woodpecker feathers. 45″ long. For the White Deerskin ceremony. Lent by the Museum of the American Indian, Heye Foundation, New York. (15/1877)

tasks. Making the baskets which were used in every phase of life was another laborious, time-consuming duty. But these labors were relieved by many ceremonial and social activities. In the redwood plank houses of the North, the domed earth lodges of the central tribes and the reed huts of the southerners, ceremonies of great beauty and complexity were performed. Salmon runs in the rivers meant jollification for every one; and for hours the young people would listen to the old men telling tales handed down from their fathers.

Despite a multiplicity of languages and customs, the Seed Gatherers of the Far West have one factor in common, the extensive development of basket making, and in this they excel the tribes of any other region of America. Baskets have been made in every size from that of a pinhead to ten or twelve feet in circumference, and in dozens of shapes which show extraordinary symmetry and refinement. Stitches may be as numerous as sixty to the inch. Dozens of kinds of plant roots, stems, barks and leaves are used. Some of the more common are black fern roots or stems, red barks of the redbud and tree-yucca, white willow twigs and tule roots, brown marsh grass root, and mottled yellow stems of the juncus rush. Beads and colored bird feathers decorated baskets of the Pomo tribe. Perhaps the most surprising use for baskets was for cooking; food and cold water placed in them were boiled by dropping in red-hot stones.

In the manufacture of their baskets the California Indians enjoy two major techniques

Fig. 55. A Yurok twined basket of white grass, black maidenhair fern, yellow porcupine quills and brown spruce root. 7½″ high, 5½″ in diameter. Lent by the Denver Art Museum, Denver. (YKa-13-P)

called twining and coiling. Twined baskets have vertical ribs arranged like the spokes of a wheel (Fig. 55). Coiled baskets have parallel horizontal ridges (Fig. 58). In the northern quarter of the state only twining is done; immediately south both twining and coiling are used. The remainder of the state makes only coiled ware.

Basket shapes and color combinations vary throughout the state. Designs also vary, though the triangle is the basis of nearly all of them. In the area of twining in the north, most baskets have either a glossy white background with red or black designs, or designs in glossy white on brown. The design elements are inclined to be small. Globular, hemispherical and conical shapes predominate. The area where both twining and coiling are done produces baskets with brown or white backgrounds and either black or red designs, some with white

Fig. 56. Pomo man's feather ornaments made of engraved crane wing bones and several kinds of colored feathers. The upright object is a hairpin and the others are ear ornaments. (11/9248) 18½″ long; (16/1176) each 10½″ long. Lent by the Museum of the American Indian, Heye Foundation, New York.

trimming. The patterns are usually bold and move in diagonals. Flattened globes, shallow trays and wide-mouthed bowls are the common shapes. One tribe in this area, the Pomo, often cover their baskets with colorful bird feathers.

In the southeastern quarter of the state the usual forms are deep wide-mouthed bowls, flat trays, and jars with very flat, square-cut shoulders often trimmed with black feathers or tufts of red yarn. In the northern part of this area the background is a light tan with horizontal designs in black and red, while in the southern part, the background is white and the red and black patterns are vertical, diagonal or horizontal. Basketry from the southwestern corner of the state may easily be recognized by its glossy, mottled yellow-brown background with patterns in black. There has been no basketry in the west central area for a long period.

Pottery was not made in California except in the extreme south. Elsewhere, vessels of basketry or stone were used. The mild climate made the production of clothing almost unnecessary. In certain parts of northern California, ornamental featherwork reached a very high stage of artistry, one not exceeded elsewhere among United States Indians (Figs. 56 and 57). In the redwood country there was some carving in wood and elkhorn. As the makers and users of money, certain California tribes went further than did any other Indian group. Using dentalium shells, shell beads of several types, red woodpecker scalps, magnesite cylinders and great blades of chipped red or black obsidian as symbols of value, they developed a financial system which played a great part in their lives.

The gentle character of most California Indians made them particularly easy victims of the invading white man. Since the Indians had no common language and

Fig. 57. Pomo feather basket. 7″ in diameter. Lent by the University of Pennsylvania Museum, Philadelphia. (NA 8268)

Fig. 58. A Washo coiled basket made by Dat-so-la-lee, one of the few Indian women whose names have become known because of the perfection of their work. 7³⁄₁₆″ high, 10″ in diameter. Lent by the University of Pennsylvania Museum, Philadelphia. (38-16-1)

no system of organizing the tribes into a defensive confederacy, few were able to resist attacks with much success. Some gathered around the missions, but the unfamiliar food and ways of living played havoc with their numbers, despite the good intentions of the Spanish missionaries. Those that lived in the mining areas were often hunted and killed like rabbits by the ruthless miners. As a result, we find here the greatest proportional decline in Indian population anywhere in the United States. From perhaps one hundred and fifty thousand, the Indians decreased to the twenty-five thousand living today in about ninety small settlements scattered from one end of the state to the other. The white man's clothing has been adopted by all California tribes for everyday use. Complete adoption of the white man's material culture is retarded only by the extreme poverty of the tribes and by the lack of opportunity typical of all under-privileged groups. Nevertheless, dances and ceremonies that bring out the most elaborate costumes are held from time to time in many places in California. The best proof that the tribal cultures of California are alive is the fact that basketry is still made in almost every section of the state, and that its quality is often as fine as that of the best pieces from old collections (Fig. 58).

Living Traditions: The Seed Gatherers of the Far West

The Hunters of the Plains

The horseback-riding nomads of the western Plains have cap-
tured a larger share of the world's interest than any other
Indians. Their fierce resistance to the white invaders, their
famed horsemanship and their colorful costumes are so familiar that many people think of all Indians as dashing raiders
on horseback, dressed in fringed buckskin and flowing war
bonnets. Actually, this picture fits only the Plains tribes, who
never constituted more than one-fifth of the Indian population of the United States and did not develop the best-
known aspects of their culture until after they got horses
from the Spanish two to three hundred years ago.

In pre-horse days most of the Plains tribes lived in fairly

Fig. 59. Area inhabited by the
Hunters of the Plains.

Fig. 60. Modern Blackfoot tipis seen from the back. The outside poles are attached to the "ears"
which control the size of the smoke hole. Several painted designs can be seen.

Fig. 61. A Cheyenne parfleche, or rawhide envelope, showing a design of the abstract type painted by women. 32″ long. Collected in 1905. Lent by Herbert J. Spinden, Brooklyn, New York.

permanent villages of large, round, log and earth houses often located in wooded areas on the edge of the Plains. Food came from gardens and small corn fields, wild plants and game. Since traveling meant walking with only dogs for pack animals, the tribes stayed fairly close to home except for seasonal hunting expeditions for buffalo, elk, antelope and deer.

This settled village life was changed almost overnight by the coming of the horse. The speedy mobility made possible by riding opened up for the Plains Indians a new and exciting world of war, of easy unhampered travel over vast areas and of efficient hunting of the buffalo which roamed in countless millions over the Plains. Glorying in their new freedom, the tribes left their old homes and took up the life of roving nomads. For such a life the Plains country was ideal, with its vast expanses stretching from the Rocky Mountains to the Mississippi and beyond, and from the Gulf of Mexico far into Canada. It was a rolling sea of grass broken only by a few ranges of hills, scattered badlands and an occasional shallow river. Real barriers to travel did not exist.

All the details of Plains Indian culture were influenced by this wandering life. The various tribes, hitherto largely unacquainted with each other and at peace, now met frequently and out of their rivalry in the hunt grew the wild and ruthless game of war they loved so well. Since they spoke different languages it was necessary to invent a sign language which could be understood all over the Plains and would be capable of exact shades of meaning. Individuality in thought and action came to be stressed to the detriment of group activities of a social and religious nature, because the tribes split into bands which assembled infrequently. Finally, hunting on horseback made it easy to obtain a plentiful supply of meat.

Fig. 62. A Sioux woman's beaded deerskin dress. The general shape was typical of all Plains women's dresses, but the type of beading is limited to a few tribes. 55″ long, 46½″ wide, 14 lbs. in weight. Late nineteenth century. Lent by the Denver Art Museum, Denver. (BS-70-P)

Living Traditions: The Hunters of the Plains

Therefore the people abandoned their old diet based mainly on plant food for a diet based on the meat of the buffalo and, to a lesser extent, the antelope and deer.

From these animals, beside food, came the raw materials necessary for a nomad's life: bones for tools, sinew for sewing, glue for mending, fuel for cooking and skins to make light and easily folded equipment. The cone-shaped skin tipi, easy to put up and adjustable to any sort of climatic condition, was the ideal dwelling for wanderers (Fig. 60). Skin clothing and bags were light and could be folded into small bundles easy to carry (Fig. 62). Rawhide, tough and unbreakable, was good for making baggage, shields and riding equipment. This use of skin influenced in turn the arts of the Plains by providing large flat surfaces which called for colorful decoration. Painting and embroidery, the best ways of decorating skins, became the great arts of the Plains tribes. Painting was traditional, as was embroidery with porcupine quills. A second type of embroidery, done with colored glass beads imported from Europe and distributed by traders, was added to these about 1800.

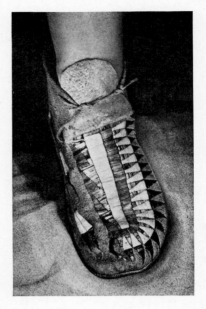

Fig. 63. A Mandan deerskin moccasin with porcupine quill embroidery. 10″ long. Lent by the Museum of the American Indian, Heye Foundation, New York. (6/326)

The rapid motion of horseback riding also encouraged the decorative use of feathers and fringes, which are at their best when stirred by the wind. This affinity of feathers and wind found its most dramatic expression in the feathered war bonnet, the badge of honor reserved for great leaders.

The painting of these tribes is one of the major developments of this art among Indians. Its origins are unknown and by the time it was first noted, about one hundred and fifty years ago, it was practiced in two well-developed styles, one used by men and one by women. Men painted vivid naturalistic representations of battles and hunting scenes on skin robes, clothing and tipis. Executed with economy of detail and with-

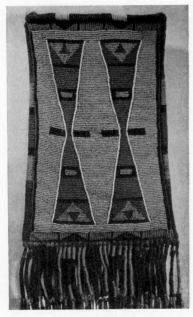

Fig. 64. A Crow beaded bag illustrating the type of abstract design developed in the late nineteenth century by the Crow and their neighbors. 9¾″ long, 6″ wide. Lent by the Denver Art Museum, Denver. (BCr-15-P)

out the use of perspective, these paintings have great animation and sensitivity. This style has passed through several phases and lives on in the water-color paintings of modern young Plains Indians. The painting done by women was restricted to abstract designs on skin robes (Fig. 65), cylindrical rawhide cases for ceremonial equipment, and the large envelope-shaped packing cases called parfleches (Fig. 61). Neither sex worked in the style of the other. The division of styles on such a basis is widespread among native races. This appears to be due to the fact that their naturalistic arts are often connected with magic and religious practices, which belong in the realm of men.

Quill embroidery (Fig. 63), the most typically Indian of all America's native crafts since it is done nowhere else in the world, is known to be of great antiquity. It has been found in a site which is several thousand years old according to geologic evidence. Its range is from Canada to the northern United States, with a southward extension along the Rocky Mountains. Porcupine quills

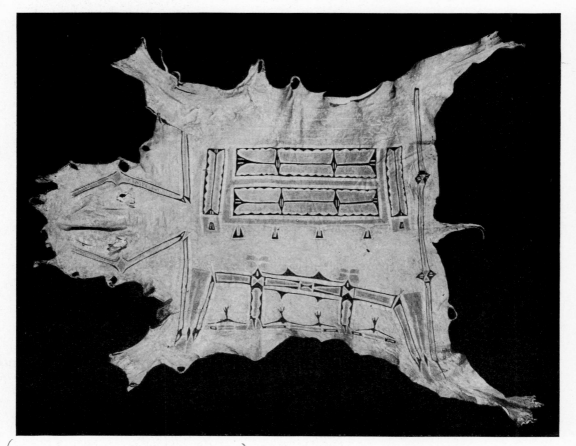

Fig. 65. A Plains child's painted skin robe. 46 " long, 36 " wide. Lent by the Field Museum of Natural History, Chicago. (12972)

Living Traditions: The Hunters of the Plains

take dyes well and need no preliminary treatment other than being softened with water and then flattened. The flattened, sewn quills present a smooth, glossy surface like that of straw. This ancient craft is practiced in many techniques and design styles. On the Plains abstract patterns prevail, though floral designs from the eastern tribes have been taken up to some extent.

Beadwork began on the Plains about 1800, but because of the scarcity and large size of the early beads its development was rather slight until about 1850. At that time quantities of very small beads became available and the craft progressed rapidly. Its best period was between 1870 and 1890. There are several basic techniques and a number of regional styles. The old traditional designs consisted of angular abstractions taken over from quillwork, but floral designs have become increasingly common among some Plains tribes. While beadwork was not restricted to the Plains, it certainly found its fullest expression there (Fig. 64).

Of all the Indian civilizations in the United States, that of the Plains people both gained and suffered most at the hands of the white invader. Two hundred years after Europeans gave the Indians the horses that made it possible for them to create one of the great hunting cultures of the world, Americans ruthlessly destroyed the buffalo herds and so robbed the Indians of the very basis on which their new life had been built. The tragic consequences of the rapid extermination of the great herds were felt in every aspect of Plains culture. Within less than one generation the people were reduced from a life of abundance to hopeless famine. They found themselves without the raw materials needed for almost every product used in their daily lives and even their beliefs and traditions lost validity, since they were perfectly adapted only to a hunter's life. This catastrophe struck the Plains people three generations ago. It was followed by desperate fighting and unbelievable misery. For years many of the tribes lived on rations handed to them by the authorities, who sometimes used hunger as an easy means of pacification.

The great buffalo herds are gone today. But in spite of persecution and misery, memories of the old hunting life on the Plains survive, and its traditions, though weakened, have not been killed. With the cooperation of the Government, the Indians of the Plains, some seventy-five thousand in number, are now rebuilding their lives around the resources of a new era. Their arts still reflect the old life and will probably continue to do so until their thoughts and concepts have become adjusted to the new order. The scarcity of raw material and the general adoption of white man's clothing for everyday wear have reduced the volume of production considerably. But many festive occasions, whether staged for the benefit of Indians or whites, still demand handmade traditional clothing and equipment, and these are often used as gifts from the maker to other members of the tribe. Such gift articles are usually excellent in design and workmanship and reveal a vitality and strength that promise to survive no matter how much the new life of these people may modify the style of their future work.

Living Traditions: The Hunters of the Plains

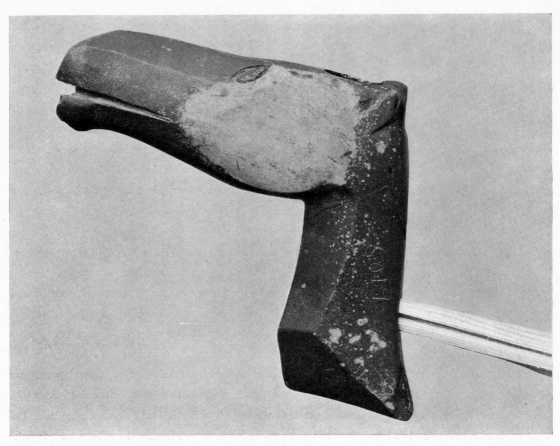

Stone Pipe Bowl, Central Plains. 4⅛″ high, 4⅛″ long. Lent by the United States National Museum, Washington, D. C. (6019)

The bowl of his pipe offered the Plains Indian his only opportunity for stone carving. Ordinarily he made plain L- or T-shaped bowls. But occasionally someone, like the unknown artist who produced this bowl, had the imagination and independence to create a true piece of sculpture. The blotch on the cheek of the horse's head is an imperfection in the stone.

The material, catlinite or pipestone, is found in many places, and ranges in color from cherry red to pale buff. When first quarried, pipestone is soft enough to be carved with a knife but hardens soon after exposure to the air. The red variety was preferred by most Plains Indians.

Pipes were used for many purposes among Indians, some in tribal ceremonies, others in private rites and many for pleasure alone. Hence it is an error to call all by the common title "peace pipe." The smoking of tobacco originated among the Indians and was closely connected in many cases with their religious beliefs. Collected before 1868 by the War Department on the Upper Missouri.

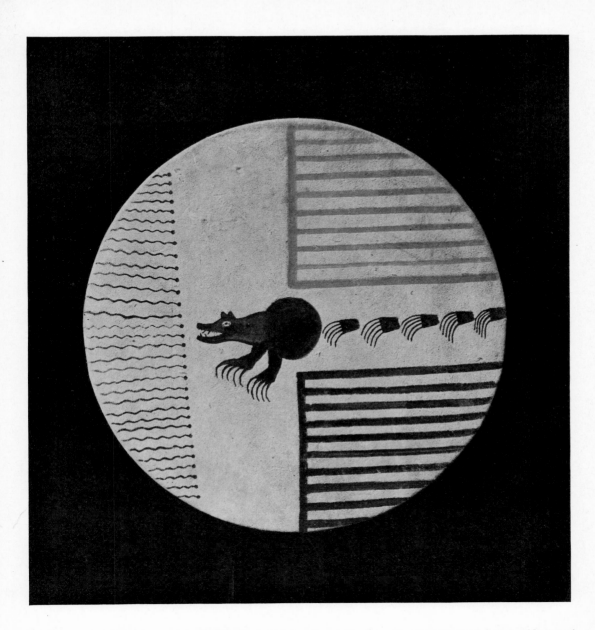

Painted Shield Cover, Kiowa, Oklahoma. 20″ in diameter. Lent by the United States National Museum, Washington, D. C. (229889)

The designs on Plains shields were believed to contain such magical power that they, rather than the shields themselves, were the real means of protection. The designs were received in visions. The red and black one shown here depicts a bear charging out between clouds toward a row of flying bullets, leaving footprints behind him. Collected in 1909 by James Mooney in Oklahoma.

Living Traditions: The Hunters of the Plains **149**

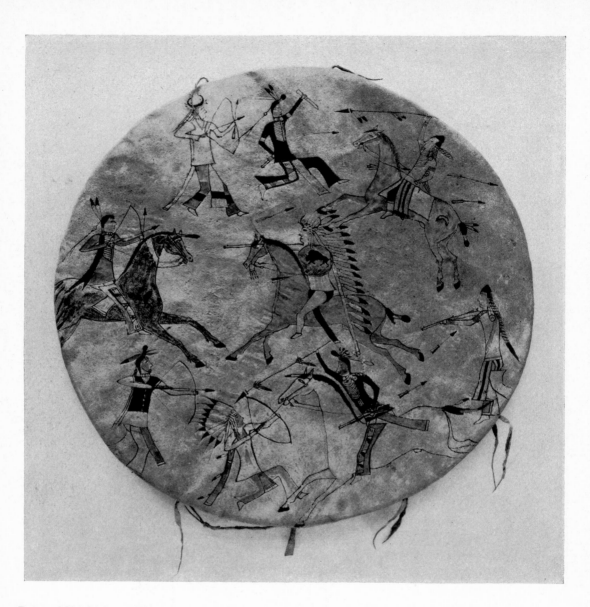

Painted Shield Cover, Sioux, South Dakota. 22¼″ in diameter. Lent by the Museum of the American Indian, Heye Foundation, New York. (6/2195)

Many representations of war and hunting scenes were painted on the Plains in the nineteenth century. The cover pictured here and the robe on page 37 are excellent examples of this school. Men were the artists, for painting by women has always been restricted to abstract design.

A fight between Sioux and Crow is depicted. The central mounted warrior shows the manner of using a shield. Made in the mid-nineteenth century. Collected before 1917.

Calumet or Medicine Pipe, Crow, Montana. 33″ long. Lent by the Denver Art Museum, Denver. (PiCr-1-P)

This pipe is an example of the most elaborately decorated and ceremonially important of the many kinds of Indian tobacco-smoking devices. The name *calumet* is usually applied to such pipes. It is derived through French from the Latin word for *reed* and refers to the slender stem.

The seventeenth century French explorers of the upper Mississippi Valley found an Indian cult of friendship which was symbolized by great feathered pipes. The idea spread widely among Middle Western tribes and out on the Plains. There, however, the pipes came to be focal points of individual rituals rather than symbols of a widespread belief. Made in the mid-nineteenth century.

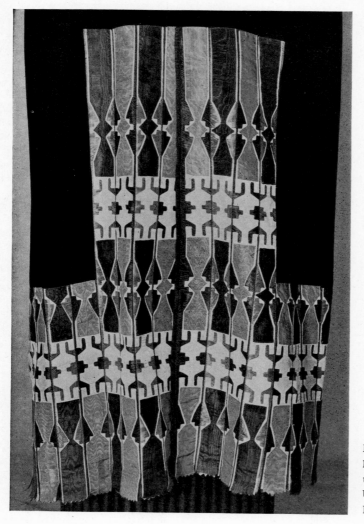

Ribbonwork Cloak, Osage, Oklahoma. 70″ long, 61″ wide. Lent by the Indian Arts and Crafts Board, United States Department of the Interior.

Appliqué work with bright silk ribbons obtained from traders has been done by the Great Lakes and Mississippi Valley tribes for at least one hundred and fifty years. It is still produced in quantity. The designs are derived from those used in two old native techniques, porcupine quill embroidery and birch bark engraving. Of the many skin and cloth articles trimmed with ribbon the largest and most spectacular is the type of woman's broadcloth cloak illustrated here. Collected in 1938 by Alice Marriott in Oklahoma.

The Woodsmen of the East

Some of our best-known national legends have as their heroes or villains Indians belonging to one or another of the many tribes which once lived in the heavily forested area east of the Mississippi. Pocahontas, the savior of Captain John Smith, was a Virginia Indian. Manhattan Indians were the victims of the shrewd Dutch in the sale of Manhattan Island. The starving Pilgrims were taught how to plant corn by Aspinet, the friendly Nauset sachem. Mohawks and Mohicans still live in the novels of Cooper, and our histories give many pages to Pontiac, the Ottawa, and Tecumseh, the Shawnee.

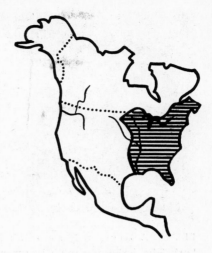

Fig. 67. Area inhabited by the Woodsmen of the East.

These familiar stories symbolize the long and difficult relations of the Eastern Woodland Indians with the white man, relations which influenced Indian life more in the Woodlands than anywhere else. The tragic story is full of broken promises, massacres on both sides, the forcible removal of entire tribes and bitter conflicts over possession of the land.

The wealth of this region lay in its forest, which even today, despite the inroads of our civilization, covers much of the East. The influence of the forest and the watercourses was felt in every detail of Indian life. Especially evident was this influence on the methods of travel. The density of forest growth made horseback riding almost impossible. But travel by canoe on the hundreds of streams and lakes was easy and quick, and from the flexible bark of birch or elm, light, fast canoes could always be made. In the South, where birch and elm did not grow, the tribes used canoes hewn from single logs.

Fig. 68. An Iroquois mask of braided corn husks worn during the curing rites of the Husk Face Society.

Dozens of tribes lived in the eastern states. Though their cultures were all conditioned by life in the forest they spoke many languages and developed different ways of life. The tribes may best be divided geographically into three large groups: the Iroquois of New York State and vicinity; the Algonquin tribes which surrounded the Iroquois on all sides; and the tribes of the South.

The Iroquois are the best known of these groups because of their remarkable organization, the League of the Six Nations. This was a plan of representative government under a constitution, founded about 1570, and was far in advance of

Fig. 69. A Montagnais box of birch bark. The design was made by scraping. 11¼" high, 8" long, 6¾" wide. Lent by the Denver Art Museum, Denver. (CMg-3-P)

any other Indian political system. Due to the strength of this unified organization the Iroquois did not suffer so much at the hands of the whites as the other eastern tribes and today they still live in their original homeland.

Like most of their neighbors the Iroquois were both hunters and farmers. In clearings scattered through the forest they built their villages of long houses—gabled frames of poles sheathed with elm bark—and cultivated their fields of corn, beans and squash. Their original rather scant garments of skin were soon replaced by those of cloth obtained from traders, as was the case with the eastern tribes generally. In their crafts they strove for simple practicability more than for dramatic effects. An exception to this rule are their masks of carved wood (page 12) and woven corn husks (Fig. 68) used by the medicine man. Their embroidery with porcupine quills or white beads is unequalled in Indian art for delicate grace.

The Algonquin tribes, whose territory surrounded the Iroquois, consist of three great divisions. One was in the Great Lakes region, the second filled all New England and the third stretched down the Atlantic coast as far as Virginia. These people lived in small villages of wigwams, dome-shaped huts of poles covered with bark, rush matting or grass. Algonquin food was much like that of the Iroquois in its use of corn and game. Fish was an important food and the Great Lakes tribes had in addition wild rice and maple sugar. Algonquin crafts are more richly developed than those of the Iroquois. The northern Algonquin are the great users of birch bark among Indians and from it make dwellings, canoes and many household utensils. Weaving is represented by flat bags and braided sashes now made with commercial wool yarn but formerly woven with basswood or nettle fiber and buffalo wool. Beadwork, both sewn and woven, and quillwork are highly developed, and around the Great Lakes silk appliqué embroidery has been an important craft for at least one hundred and fifty years. Wood is carved into bowls, spoons and cradles.

Until about 1700 pottery making was widely distributed

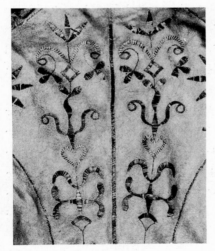

Fig. 70. Detail of the porcupine quill embroidery on a Chippewa elkskin coat of the early nineteenth century. 43" long, 21" wide. Lent by the Denver Art Museum, Denver. (VCe-1-P)

among both Iroquois and Algonquin. All pots were unpainted. Both groups also took over silverworking from the early settlers and developed their own types of metalworking.

The Algonquin have three major design styles. Around the Great Lakes there is a simple, angular geometric style which has been largely superseded by one in which graceful plant forms appear (Fig. 69). In New England and north of it is found the "double curve" style (Fig. 71).

The Algonquin lacked the unified political organization of the Iroquois and were still living in many semi-independent bands when the pressure of white expansion began. As a result they suffered much more than the Iroquois. Most of the Atlantic seaboard tribes either became extinct or were moved to Middle Western reservations. Only the Great Lakes tribes have been able to stay in their former homes, and even some of them are now in the Mississippi Valley and Oklahoma.

Fig. 71. A Micmac hood of blue cloth embroidered with glass beads. 15″ long, 7″ wide. Lent by the Museum of American Indian, Heye Foundation, New York. (17/6432)

The southern Indians were very numerous and in their semitropical surroundings had developed in prehistoric times one of the most unusual and colorful of Indian cultures. Some details of this culture have been suggested on page 62. However, it offered slight resistance to the introduction of most European ideas and trade goods. The old aboriginal types of clothing, housing and manufactures, except basketry, disappeared rather quickly and were replaced by those of European style or by local adaptations of foreign ideas. The characteristic regional design style based on the scroll survived only in beaded decorations on cloth (Fig. 72). The large tribes became involved in the struggle between European nations, and later the survivors became further involved in the expansion of Americans to the west. Eventually they were driven to their present homes in Oklahoma.

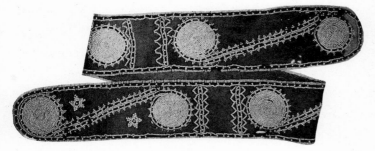

Fig. 72. A Choctaw beaded belt. Collected in 1812. 49½″ long, 3½″ wide. Lent by the Denver Art Museum, Denver. (BChe-1-P)

With the exception of the Florida Seminole most eastern tribes have adjusted themselves exceedingly well to the manner of living of their white neighbors. Most tribes have, however, retained many of their arts and much of their social and ceremonial life.

Living Traditions: The Woodsmen of the East

War Club, Iroquois, Pennsylvania. 20″ long, 1 lb. 12 oz. in weight. Lent by the Denver Art Museum, Denver. (L36-211)

The ball-headed wooden club was the classic weapon in the hand-to-hand forest warfare of the eastern tribes. Following the widespread introduction of the European metal hatchet, called tomahawk after an Indian word for war club, the ball club became less popular for actual use, surviving principally as a formal element of Indian full dress paraphernalia.

Woodworking among the Woodland tribes was restricted largely to the making of bows, paddles, clubs, masks, bowls and spoons. Before metal tools were obtained, carving was done by charring the wood and scraping off the burned sections with stone or shell tools. Metal made woodworking easier and the craft reached its height in the eighteenth and early nineteenth centuries.

The maple wood club illustrated here is one of the finest known. It was found in the late eighteenth century near the site of Braddock's defeat by the French and Indians in 1755 and was presumably used in that battle. The animal head on the handle may indicate the clan of its owner.

Living Traditions: The Woodsmen of the East

Wooden Mask, Iroquois, New York. 10¼″ high, 6½″ wide. Lent by the Denver Art Museum, Denver. (NSen-8-P)

Wooden masks were widely used in the northeastern United States, especially among the Iroquois. Only in Alaska and British Columbia are they found in comparable quantity and variety. In the Southwest, the other great center of masking, skin and cloth are the traditional materials.

The preliminary carving of Iroquois masks is done on living trees because the Indians wish the masks to be alive also. They represent various mythical beings and are still made and worn by the members of doctors' societies.

Twisted and exaggerated features and a profusion of wrinkles are typical of Iroquois masks. They are usually painted black or red and have hair made of horsetails. The oriental appearance of the mask illustrated here is entirely coincidental. Early twentieth century. Collected in 1920 by A. G. Heath on the Cattaraugas Reservation, New York.

Living Traditions: The Woodsmen of the East

Birch Bark Box, Cree, South Central Canada. 11″ long, 6″ wide, 7½″ high. Lent by the Denver Art Museum, Denver. (CWC-1-P)

Such boxes for general household use are made by cutting a sheet of bark to a pattern, folding it into shape and sewing it with spruce root. The designs are produced by scraping away the white outside layer of bark to disclose the brown layer beneath.

Birch bark is of the greatest importance to the tribes living in the extreme northern United States and throughout much of Canada and Alaska. Dwellings, canoes and much household and food-gathering equipment are made with it. Because birch bark is always available and easy to work these tribes make no pottery and very few baskets.

The animal and plant forms (especially the latter) in which the region abounds are the chief source of the designs created on birch bark. Natural forms are often highly conventionalized in this region, and the realism of the bear, beaver and caribou on this box are exceptional. Made about 1890 and collected in 1925 by A. G. Heath.

Bark Fiber Bag, Menominee, Wisconsin. 14¾″ wide, 9½″ high. Lent by the American Museum of Natural History, New York. (50.1/6862)

This is a bag for storing or transporting ceremonial equipment. The light-colored string is made from the fibrous inner bark of the basswood tree. The dark thread is brown buffalo wool. No loom is used. The warp or foundation threads are hung over a crossbar and the weft or binding threads are interwoven by a weaving technique called twining. Women are the makers.

Bags of this shape and character are the principal woven product of the Great Lakes tribes and are largely restricted to them. Various bark and plant fibers are the standard sources of cord and thread throughout the East. Wool and cotton were introduced there by Europeans.

The design on the bag illustrated here represents the Underground Panther, a mythological creature of the region, easily recognizable by its very long tail. Representations of legendary beings appear on ceremonial bags, while those for general use show only abstract designs. Early nineteenth century. Collected in 1901 by Alanson Skinner.

Living Traditions: The Woodsmen of the East **159**

Beaded Bag, Ojibwa, Wisconsin. 42″ long, 17″ wide. Lent by the Denver Art Museum, Denver. (BOj-2-Ex.)

Bags of this type are worn today by the Ojibwa as symbols of wealth and social position and have no practical use. They have evolved, however, from a thoroughly practical bag, the small bullet pouch of early pioneer times.

The patterns are examples of the modern phase of a design style which contains both European and Indian elements. The use of plant forms is Indian, but their rather realistic treatment is the result of early French influence. The bag illustrated here was made about 1875 and collected in 1910 by the Milwaukee Public Museum.

The Fishermen of the Northwest Coast

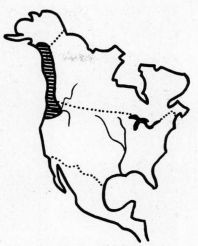

The sea and the trees of their native land are the foundations of life for the Fishermen of the Northwest Coast. They live along a thousand miles of forest-covered coast stretching north from Puget Sound in the northwestern corner of Washington to Yakutat Bay in southern Alaska.

Offshore are hundreds of hilly islands large and small. Almost from the water's edge high mountains rise, cutting off the coast from the interior. Both islands and mountains are covered with dense forests of giant trees, red and yellow cedars and Sitka spruce. The whole scene is veiled in drifting

Fig. 73. Area inhabited by the Fishermen of the Northwest Coast.

fog and rain. The sea swarms with fish; game and fur-bearing land and sea animals abound; and a profusion of undergrowth on the land produces many berries.

Because of the sea which touches every village, and the forests which provide an endless supply of easily worked wood, these tribes became the greatest navigators and woodworkers of all American Indians, and built a civilization which reflected perfectly the abundance of nature engendered by the mild, damp climate. Everything was done on a grand scale. The houses and canoes were immense. The wealth of the great families was counted in lavish quantities of furs, blankets, slaves and scores of beautifully made wooden boxes, horn dishes and copper shields. Beside the dark sea and forest there developed an art in which men, animals and gods were inextricably mingled in strange, intricate carvings and paintings. Religion and mythology found their outlet in vast ceremonies in which fantastically masked figures enacted tense, wild dramas.

Fig. 74. An Indian-made model canoe. 30″ long, 6″ wide. Large canoes were sixty feet or more long. Lent by the Museum of the American Indian, Heye Foundation, New York. (6/9469)

Living Traditions: The Fishermen of the Northwest Coast   **161**

Fig. 75. A Tlinkit house and totem pole. Houses of this type were about forty by fifty feet in size and were made of handhewn cedar planks. The photograph was taken in 1899.

The origins of this civilization are puzzling. There are indications that it is not very old compared with other native cultures, but we know that its elements were already well established at the time of its discovery in 1774. Early contacts with the white man stimulated and increased its development in many ways. The fur trade brought great wealth to a people who had high regard for material things, and caused a tremendous outburst of the love of display that was always characteristic of these proud and warlike tribes. Metal tools, unknown before the Russians came two hundred years ago, made it possible for the carvers to develop their craft to a degree unattainable with their old tools of bone, stone or jade. Carved posts of modest size grew into gigantic totem poles towering over the houses to proclaim the wealth and family pride of their owners in a dramatic manner that is one of the basic characteristics of Northwest Coast art.

The giant red cedar tree was and still is the greatest source of raw material. Its wood went into houses, totem poles, canoes, boxes, masks and other ceremonial equipment, and into innumerable smaller objects. Its bark was woven into mats to line the walls of the vast, drafty houses, and into the everyday clothing of the people. The long slender roots were woven into baskets of many shapes, brightly colored with plant dyes (Fig. 76). Even in mountain goat wool garments, cedar bark had a place as the warp strings.

The women wove colorful mountain goat wool garments on which were emblazoned the intricate heraldic designs of the noble families (Fig. 77). Commercial wool blankets

Fig. 76. A Tlinkit basket. 15″ high. Lent by the American Museum of Natural History, New York.

were embroidered with white buttons or with dentalium shells (Fig. 78). The women also made baskets with many-colored geometric designs. The men hammered copper into ornaments and "coppers," big shield-shaped objects highly prized as symbols of wealth. There were small bone, stone and ivory carvings such as dagger handles, magicians' charms and women's jewelry. Skillfully wrought and engraved silver bracelets were made from coins. Painted designs could be seen on everything from immense house fronts (Fig. 75) to small objects for personal use. The horns of mountain goats were boiled soft, shaped in wooden molds and carved into dishes and spoons.

Taking advantage of their old native skills, the Indians of Alaska are adjusting themselves rapidly to new conditions.

Fishing is still their main occupation, but the fishermen sell their catch to American canneries, and powerboats have replaced the canoes. Today many old traditions have disappeared. Indian villages have been abandoned in favor of the towns. The population, formerly about sixty thousand, declined to about twenty thousand, but is now increasing.

The old customs and crafts were discouraged by the intolerant attitude of most of the early white settlers toward all manifestations of Indian culture.

In spite of these unfavorable conditions the arts of the Northwest Coast still survive and show signs of fresh vigor. A new recognition of their value by the authorities and the public has released their dormant strength and produced work of excellent quality.

Fig. 77. A Chilkat blanket-cape woven in 1938. The colors are the black, white, yellow and green always used in Chilkat textiles. 32″ long, 40″ wide. Most of these capes are much larger. Lent anonymously.

Fig. 78. A Haida shirt of commercial cloth embroidered with dentalium shells. The design is a beaver. 45¼″ long, 31¼″ wide. Lent by the Museum of the American Indian, Heye Foundation, New York. (14/9606)

Living Traditions: The Fishermen of the Northwest Coast

Wooden Mask, Cowichan, Vancouver Island. 19½″ high, 11¾″ wide. Lent by the Denver Art Museum, Denver. (NCow-1-P)

This mask represents a mythical being which descended from the sky to live in the waters of lakes, and came to be the spirit protector of certain noble families. The angularity, simplification of form and use of parallel grooves which appear on the mask are features characteristic of Salish wood-carving. When worn, the mask is encircled by a ruff of swan feathers and sea lion whiskers. Collected in 1935 by G. T. Emmons at Duncan, Vancouver Island, British Columbia.

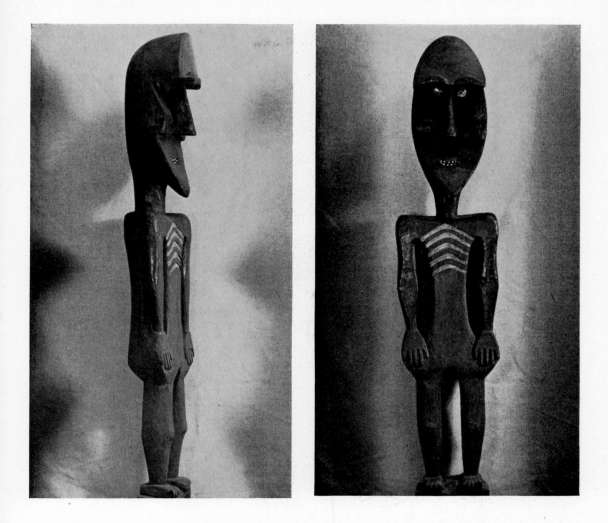

Wooden Figure, Salish, Northwestern Washington. 36″ high. Lent by the American Museum of Natural History, New York. (16/6946)

The Salish tribes in the general Puget Sound region formerly made such figures in connection with their religious beliefs. The figures are of various sizes, but all show the same style of carving. This style is unrelated to that of the rest of the Northwest Coast, illustrated on pages 166–184, and appears to belong to an older, more rudimentary school of sculpture.

The figures represent spirits controlled by the medicine men. They are set up around the shaman's home during his rites, or used as grave markers. Smaller carved figures are used as charms. Collected in 1899 by H. I. Smith among the Quinault at Bay Center.

Living Traditions: The Fishermen of the Northwest Coast

Wooden Figure, Haida, Northern British Columbia. 16″ high. Lent by the American Museum of Natural History, New York. (16/396)

A dancing medicine man is represented here. The carving was made for sale to white men in the early days of the souvenir market. Yet it is executed with the formalized realism traditional in the region. Collected about 1880.

Slate Carving, "The Bear Mother," Haida, British Columbia. 5½″ long. Lent by the United States National Museum, Washington, D. C. (73117)

Like so much Northwest Coast sculpture this small figure illustrates a story. A party of women went to gather berries in the forest. While they were at work some bears appeared and were mocked by the women. The bears became enraged and killed all of the berry pickers but one. She was carried away to the bears' home and married their king. When her child was born it had human form but the instincts of its animal father. Sometime later hunters saw what they thought was a bear in a tree, but the creature convinced them she was the woman who had been stolen and begged them to take her back to the village. This was done, and from the Bear Mother all members of the Bear clan are believed to be descended.

The carving shows the mother writhing in agony while nursing her fierce, unnatural offspring. The figurine is one of the most celebrated produced by the Indian sculptors of the Northwest Coast, largely because it displays a personal emotion foreign to traditional Indian work.

The Bear Mother was carved by Skaowskeay, a Haida Indian of Skidegate, in the summer of 1883. It was not completely finished by him, for the final polishing was done by another Haida sculptor named Kit-Elswa, while making the return voyage from Skidegate to Vancouver with the collector.

The figure was collected for the Smithsonian Institution in September, 1883, by James G. Swan. It is carved in a massive black slate found only on the Queen Charlotte Islands.

Wooden War Helmet, Tlinkit, Southeastern Alaska. 12″ high, 13″ in diameter. Lent by the American Museum of Natural History, New York. (E/453)

This is the upper part of a two-piece helmet. This type was developed, along with wood and hide armor, for the hand-to-hand fighting with club and knife common on the Northwest Coast in the early nineteenth century. The lower part of the helmet is a broad collar encircling the neck. Traces of red paint remain on the weathered grey wood.

The face on the helmet is a carefully executed portrait of an actual person afflicted with a partial facial paralysis. The twisting of the features, characteristic of the disease, is indicated with a degree of realism rare in Indian art. Only the formalized treatment of the eyebrows recalls the stylization of natural forms so dominant in Northwest Coast art and illustrated on the following pages. Indians rarely executed portraits, but this helmet proves that they were well within the capabilities of the native artist. Early nineteenth century. Collected about 1885 by G. T. Emmons at Chilkoot, Alaska.

Wooden Mask, Haida, British Columbia. 9″ high. Lent by the American Museum of Natural History, New York. (16/362)

This mask represents a type of Indian work which, though made primarily for sale, was true to the traditional artistic standards of the region. It represents a girl wearing a labret in her lower lip. Such ornaments were commonly worn by women of the Northwest Coast tribes.

The production of articles for sale to white visitors is not a recent development among the Northwest Coast tribes, for it was well established by 1860. Collected about 1880 by J. W. Powell.

Living Traditions: The Fishermen of the Northwest Coast   **169**

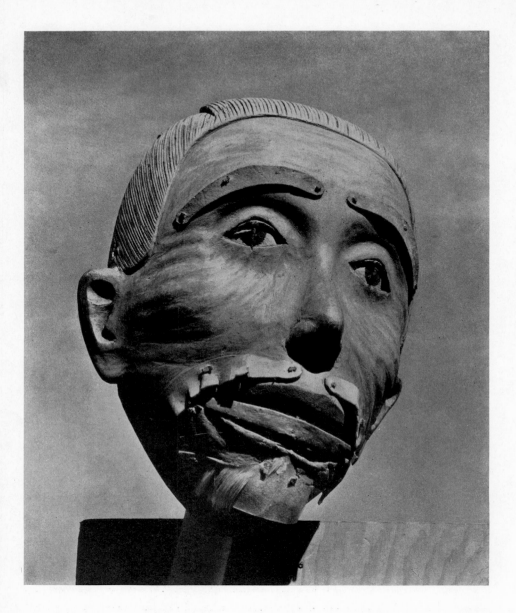

Wooden Mask, Haida, British Columbia. 10″ high. Lent by the University of California, Berkeley.

In the wintertime the Northwest Coast tribes were accustomed to present dramatic spectacles which were for entertainment only. Many of the performers wore masks to heighten the power of their acting. Some of the most effective masks had movable features like the eyelids and lower lip in the mask illustrated here. The strips over the eyes and around the mouth formerly were covered with white hair, to supplement the remarkable realism of the carving.

Living Traditions: The Fishermen of the Northwest Coast

Wooden Mask, Nootka, Vancouver Island. 12″ high, 8″ wide. Lent by the Field Museum of Natural History, Chicago. (85843)

This mask represents a wild man of the mountains. The character appears in the winter dances of the tribes. He usually acts as a medicine man, and suffers sometimes from attacks of frenzy, breaks away from the other dancers and rushes about destroying property. The mask is trimmed with cedar bark. This material is widely used on the Northwest Coast for making household and ceremonial equipment. Collected in 1903 by C. F. Newcombe on Vancouver Island.

Living Traditions: The Fishermen of the Northwest Coast

Wooden Mask, Kwakiutl, Vancouver Island. 12″ high. Lent by the American Museum of Natural History, New York. (16/692)

Some Northwest Coast masks were carved in the likenesses of spirits or mythical beings who were believed to be ancestors of the various families. To suggest the unhuman character of these ancestors, the masks representing them were often given features which, though basically human, were exaggerated in a grotesque manner. Collected in 1894 by Franz Boas in Vancouver.

Wooden Mask, Tsimshian, British Columbia. 9″ high, 8″ wide. Lent by the Museum of the American Indian, Heye Foundation, New York. (3/4678)

The sculpture of each Northwest Coast tribe has characteristics which make it distinctive, though the work of all tribes is united by a common technique and design style. The best Tsimshian carving has great sensitiveness and subtlety, compared with the massive power of Haida work and the bold elaborations of the Kwakiutl. Collected in 1914 by George G. Heye in England.

Living Traditions: The Fishermen of the Northwest Coast **173**

Wooden Figure, Kwakiutl, Vancouver Island. 5′ 7″ high. Lent by the Museum of the American Indian, Heye Foundation, New York. (6/8754)

The Kwakiutl make many more or less life-size figures of single human beings, most of them in connection with the complex ceremony called the potlatch. In this ceremony rival chiefs strove to outdo each other in displaying and giving away property in order to gain higher social rank. The figures represent the chiefs or their official speakers, and were either displayed in the houses or set up outside on posts or roof tops. Collected before 1917 by D. F. Tozier.

Mural Painting on Wood, Nootka, Vancouver Island. 118″ long, 68¼″ wide. Lent by the American Museum of Natural History, New York. (16.1/1892A)

This is one of a pair of partitions of the type set up inside the big plank houses of the Northwest Coast tribes. The two paintings depict an adventure of a hero named Sin-set. This section shows Lightning Snake, Wolf, and Thunderbird carrying away Killer Whale.

The boards of which the partition is made were split from red cedar logs and hewn with adzes to the required thinness of about an inch. Their surfaces show the fine ripple marks left by the adze, a typical feature of southern Northwest Coast woodwork. To the north, the adze marks were rubbed off with dogfish skin. After the boards were finished they were tied together edge to edge with cedar root cords, some of which show in the photograph.

The painting was done by a trained artist hired by the owner of the house. The brushes used were of porcupine hair set in wooden handles. Before being painted, the entire surface of the boards was given a coating of oil from salmon eggs, and the two colors were also mixed with the oil. The black is charcoal and the red is made from alder bark.

Painting is almost certainly an older art on the Northwest Coast than the sculpture for which the region is so famed. The first explorers all speak of painted house fronts, canoes and other things, but say little about carving, except of rather small objects. Painting did not die out with the development of carving but flourished with it, so any artist was both painter and sculptor. Made on Vancouver Island about 1850. Collected about 1929 by G. T. Emmons.

Living Traditions: The Fishermen of the Northwest Coast

Totem Pole, Haida, British Columbia. 30′ high. Lent by the Indian Arts and Crafts Board, United States Department of the Interior.

This thirty-foot pole was carved in 1939 at the Indian exhibit in the Federal Building at the San Francisco Exposition. The carvers were two Haida Indians, John Wallace and his son, Fred. John Wallace was eighty years old and, as the third in a line of totem pole carvers, is a complete master of all the techniques and traditions of the art. The pole was carved and painted in approximately four months.

The cedar log was placed in a horizontal position on low trestles. Before the carving began, a fairly deep hollow was made in what was to be the back of the pole, in order to lessen the risk of cracking. The major units of the design were first outlined with chalk and then roughed out with an axe. Next followed the long process of cutting away the background with adzes in order to bring out the figures of the design in relief. The final small details were carved with knives and chisels. Each of these three steps was begun at the top and carried down to the bottom. After all the carving was completed, the pole was painted with ordinary house paint.

Totem pole carving was restricted to the Northwest Coast Indians and had its fullest development in the mid-nineteenth century. It was an outgrowth of an older custom of carving house roof supports and was made possible by two influences, the large-scale introduction of metal tools into the area, and the rapid development of the Indians' wealth through the fur trade. There are no very ancient poles in existence today because they rot in the damp climate and fall to the ground in sixty to seventy years. Fallen poles were often cut up into firewood.

Totem poles are not idols and are not made to be worshipped. They either display family crests or relate family legends, and were erected as memorials to dead leaders and as symbols of family pride and wealth. It is impossible to "read" the designs because the significance of each figure is determined by the owner and not in accordance with any general system. The carver arranges the figures on a pole in accordance with his taste, and not in the order in which they appear in the story or genealogy. Even the sequence of figures on two poles telling the same story is not identical.

The pole illustrated tells a family legend. Raven dives to the bottom of the ocean, finds totem poles at the home of Killer Whale, and with the aid of various creatures brings one to the surface and gives it to the Indians.

Chilkat Blanket, Tlinkit, Southeastern Alaska. 64″ high, 54″ wide. Lent by the Field Museum of Natural History, Chicago. (19571)

Blankets of this shape and size are worn as capes by the leading members of aristocratic families, primarily as a means of displaying their owners' family crests.

The blankets are woven by women, but since women may not create designs involving life forms the blanket patterns are painted on boards by men and copied in weaving by the women. This procedure is exactly the opposite of the usual Indian practice of creating designs without the aid of previously drawn patterns. Chilkat blankets are made of mountain goat wool. Green, black, yellow and white are the conventional colors. Chilkat weavers also make shirts, kilts and leggings.

The blanket illustrated here is very unusual in design. A typical Chilkat blanket is shown on page 163. The usual Chilkat weaving technique is very tight diagonal twining, but the blanket on this page is largely made with a rather open plain twined weave.

The history of this early nineteenth century specimen is unknown. It was bought by the Field Museum from Carl Hagenbeck in 1893.

Living Traditions: The Fishermen of the Northwest Coast   177

Wooden Chest, Tlinkit, Southeastern Alaska. 21¼″ high, 33″ wide, 20″ deep. Lent by the American Museum of Natural History, New York. (E/1237)

The Northwest Coast tribes used large wooden chests to store clothing and other possessions. Their sides were usually made of one board by steaming and bending. The bottom and lid are single pieces grooved to fit the sides, to which the former is sewn with spruce roots. The white objects set in the lid of the chest illustrated here are opercula, or covers which close the openings of mollusk shells. Opercula are used as ornamental inlays on many Northwest Coast wooden objects.

The design on this chest represents an animal, shown as if split up the back and laid flat. Some parts are greatly enlarged, others are omitted and all are highly conventionalized. The face is upper center and the body is below, flanked by its hind legs. The eye-like designs in the corners are the shoulder and hip joints seen in cross section.

Many of the details of this and other carvings in the same style are standardized and drawn from bark patterns used again and again. Collected about 1890 by G. T. Emmons.

Wooden Dish, Tlinkit, Southeastern Alaska. 8″ high, 13″ square. Lent by the Taylor Museum, Colorado Springs. (XX/079)

Wooden food dishes and containers were standard equipment on the Northwest Coast. As the food contained much oil, the dishes became saturated with it and in time came to have dark, polished surfaces. The dish illustrated here, over sixty years old, still smells strongly of fish oil.

Food dishes vary widely in shape. Their forms range from plain square boxes to quite realistic representations of animals. The dish illustrated here lies somewhere between. It does not have an animal shape but its carvings and bulging sides somehow suggest a living creature. The dish was collected as an old piece in Sitka in 1883 and must therefore have been made in the mid-nine-teenth century, the best period of Northwest Coast art.

Living Traditions: The Fishermen of the Northwest Coast **179**

Horn Dish, Tlinkit, Southeastern Alaska. 10⅜″ long, 5¾″ high, 6¼″ wide. Lent by the American Museum of Natural History, New York. (19/696)

The horns of two varieties of local wild animals, the mountain goat and the mountain sheep, were widely used by the Northwest Coast tribes in the manufacture of dishes, ladles and spoons.

To prepare a mountain sheep horn for use, a number of steps are necessary. First it is boiled to make it soft and flexible. When in this condition it is straightened and a piece approximating the shape and size of the object to be made is cut out. While this is still soft it is scraped to reduce its thickness, and cut out more nearly in its final form.

The next step is to shape the roughly cut dish or spoon by placing it, still soft and flexible, in a pair of wooden molds, one of which fits snugly into the other. The horn is allowed to dry in the mold, and is removed when it has hardened in the desired shape. Finally, it is carefully trimmed and then decorated by carving.

The dish illustrated here is a superb example of horn carving. It is scraped thin enough to be translucent and shows beautiful yellow-orange mottling when held up to the light. Mountain goat horn spoons, not illustrated in this book, are black and have slender, elaborately carved handles. The uses and designs of horn objects are discussed further on the opposite page. Collected in 1885 by G. T. Emmons at Yakutat.

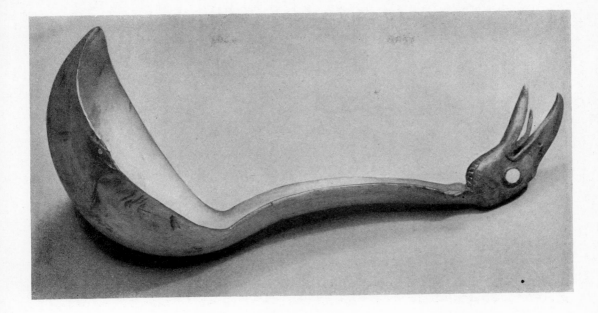

Horn Ladle, Tlinkit, Southeastern Alaska. 18″ long. Lent by the American Museum of Natural History, New York. (E/261)

Finely carved ladles, dishes and spoons of mountain sheep horn were used on the Northwest Coast in the great feasts held during the winter ceremonial season. The process of making them is described on the opposite page. They were used especially for serving and drinking the fish and animal oils which had such a favored place in the diet of these tribes. The olachen or candlefish was the prime source of oil. Its body is so rich in grease that it can be burned like a candle, hence the name. The little fish were caught in immense numbers and their oil extracted by boiling.

Because of their texture, horn dishes and ladles were especially well suited to be carved with the conventionalized animal designs of the region. But the size of horn objects usually made it impossible to represent entire creatures on them. Hence they often show a device typical of the region—that of representing some outstanding feature of each animal as a symbol of the whole. This device is illustrated by the dish on the opposite page. The carver wished to decorate this dish with two hawks. Since the symbol of a hawk is a beak curving back to touch the breast, it was only necessary for him to carve two faces having such beaks. The designs on the sides are conventionalized feathers.

The bird head illustrated on this page can be identified as a raven because of its long and relatively straight beak. It was collected about 1885 by G. T. Emmons.

Living Traditions: The Fishermen of the Northwest Coast   **181**

Wooden Rattle, Tlinkit, Southeastern Alaska. 10″ long, 9″ high. Lent by the Denver Art Museum, Denver. (QT1-23-P)

On the Northwest Coast many kinds of wooden rattles were used, two of which are the most common. One of them, illustrated here, is always in the shape of a bird; the other is globular. Both types were used by medicine men and chiefs during ceremonies.

The ordinary bird rattle is in the form of a raven bearing on its back a man, a frog and a merganser duck. The rattle shown, however, represents a crane which has on its back a land otter and her young. Since the land otter is an animal connected with witchcraft, this rattle was evidently made for a man who worked in black magic. On the crane's chest is carved the face of some other creature that cannot be identified.

The rattle is made of two pieces of wood hollowed out into thin shells and tied together at their edges. There are little pebbles inside. The crane's beak is made of ivory. The rattle is painted with the red and blue-green colors so typical of Northwest Coast art in the nineteenth century.

This rattle has an interesting history. In 1879 the late Rev. Aaron Lindsley went to Alaska to establish the first Protestant missions among the Tlinkit. So effective were his labors that he was visited by Shakes, Kadishan and other Indian leaders, and given some of their most treasured possessions as a symbol of their renunciation of pagan ways. The rattle and other things given to Mr. Lindsley had been family heirlooms of their Indian owners and must therefore date back to the early nineteenth century.

Wooden Rattle, Tlinkit, Southeastern Alaska. 10″ long with handle. Lent by the Washington State Museum, Seattle. (955)

To its Indian maker this rattle represented the front foot of a brown bear. The human face is an ornament on its sole. This is a good illustration of how racial points of view differ, for to us the rattle appears to be a face ornamented with bear claws. The bear was the family crest of Chief Shakes, the original owner of the mask. The rattle was made for use in any of the many ceremonies of the tribe. Collected before 1909 by G. T. Emmons at Fort Wrangell, Alaska.

Living Traditions: The Fishermen of the Northwest Coast   **183**

Slate Pipe Stem, Haida, British Columbia. 13″ long, 6″ wide. Lent by the Peabody Museum, Harvard University, Cambridge. (10997)

Slate carving is a specialty of the Haida Indians of the Queen Charlotte Islands. The slate, technically a carbonaceous shale, is found in only one place on the islands. It is a rather soft black stone which is quarried in quite thick pieces rather than in the thin sheets from which roofing and blackboards are made. Carving is done with steel or iron knives. Numerous objects are made, such as pipe stems like that illustrated here, models of totem poles, plates, cups, small chests and groups of human or animal figures.

Slate carvings have not been found in archaeological sites, nor are they mentioned by the explorers who first reached the Haida in 1787. Smoking was introduced at this time among the Northwest Coast tribes by Europeans, and the oldest extant slate carvings are very late eighteenth century pipe stems in the British Museum. Hence it seems likely that smoking and slate carving began about the same time.

If this is the case, it is remarkable how quickly the new art achieved the perfection shown by the British Museum pieces and others collected in the next few decades. The explanation may be that wood-carving technique was well developed already, and could easily have been adapted to the rather soft, fine grained stone.

The post-European origin of the art is further indicated by the fact that slate carvings were made largely—if not entirely—to sell to white visitors. The records of the 1838 Wilkes expedition speak of this business as a well established one, and similar comments are made by many later travelers. As time passed, the carving of slate pipes and pipe stems passed out of style and was largely replaced by the production of model totem poles. The art was at its best in the middle years of the nineteenth century. Collected in 1875 by Holmes Hinckley.

The Eskimo Hunters
of the Arctic

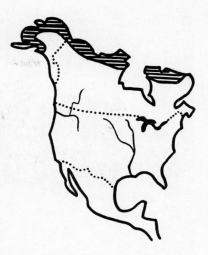

Cold, fog, snow and ice rule the world of the Eskimo. The winters are only briefly interrupted by short, warm summers. Because the climate severely limits the natural resources of the country, the people, in order to live, are forced to develop inventiveness and technical skill to a high degree.

In Alaska most of the Eskimo live in widely separated little villages on the plains of the northern and western coast. These almost treeless tundras are cut here and there by slow rivers, and by outcrops of lichen-covered boulders and scanty growths of low willows. A few bands of Eskimo still live

Fig. 79. Area inhabited by the ancient Eskimo Hunters of the Arctic.

along the mountainous, forest-covered coast of southern Alaska where the climate is less severe.

A successful adaptation to a difficult environment is the greatest achievement of the Eskimo. Since wild life is their country's only abundant resource the people depend on animals, birds and fish for most of their needs. They are eaters of meat and fish, make their clothing of furs and skins, and use animal products in building their homes. To be able to follow the game on land and sea the Eskimo invented the dogsled and the skin kayak (Fig. 82). To conquer cold and moisture they devised tightly sewn, well tailored fur clothing and garments of waterproof membrane. To make up for the lack of firewood they invented a blubber-burning stove lamp with a moss wick. Alaska Eskimo dwellings are skin tents in summer and underground huts made of driftwood and earth in winter. The snow house is not used.

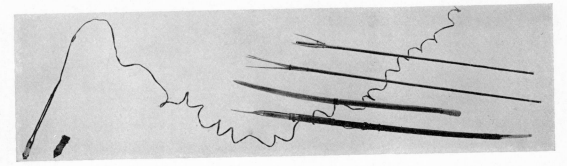

Fig. 80. Eskimo hunting weapons: harpoon line, harpoon, bird spears and ice pick to make holes for fishing. Lent by the University of California and the Denver Art Museum.

Living Traditions: The Eskimo Hunters of the Arctic

Fig. 81. An Aleut raincoat made of seal intestines. 48″ long, 36″ wide. Lent by the Peabody Museum, Harvard University. (2107)

Eskimo men are occupied with hunting and making hunting equipment (Fig. 80). Driftwood provides material for spear handles, bows and various small articles, while walrus ivory is used for objects that need to be harder and more resistant, such as spear heads and skin scrapers. Women make the fur and skin clothing (Fig. 81) and baskets. Formerly they also made a little pottery.

Ivory provides ideal material for engravings and small animal sculptures whose realism shows the Eskimo's keen powers of observation. All the playfulness and intelligence of the race are reflected in the charming and capable handling of this delicate work (Fig. 85). No other race differentiates so clearly between portrayal and artistic creation. In contrast with the lifelike animal sculptures, Eskimo masks representing spirits reveal a most daring imagination.

Half of the world's Eskimo, about nineteen thousand, are found today in Alaska. The others live in Greenland, Canada and Siberia. All are united by a common language of great complexity.

Fig. 82. A model, made by an Eskimo, of a kayak. 20½″ long, 6″ high. Lent by the Museum of the American Indian, Heye Foundation, New York. (5/3610)

Living Traditions: The Eskimo Hunters of the Arctic

Wooden Mask, Southwestern Alaska. 12½″ long. Lent by the Museum of the American Indian, Heye Foundation, New York. (12/910)

This mask represents a seal and its inua, or spirit, the latter being the half face on the left. The belief that all living things have a spirit within them which may make its appearance at will is a common one among the Eskimo. But the division of one mask into two distinct halves to symbolize this idea is very unusual. Collected before 1923 at Good News Bay.

Living Traditions: The Eskimo Hunters of the Arctic

Wooden Mask, Southwestern Alaska. 18″ high. Lent by the Museum of the American Indian, Heye Foundation, New York. (12/925)

Certain Eskimo masks are used in contests between Eskimo villages in which the players try to provoke laughter through comic gestures and the use of masks with humorous features. It is possible that the mask shown here was made for this purpose. Collected before 1923 at Good News Bay.

Wooden Mask, Southwestern Alaska. 13¾" high, 5" wide. Lent by René d'Harnoncourt, Washington, D. C.

Very little is known about the many types of Eskimo masks except that they are either connected with magic or made for entertainment at purely social functions. The seal mask illustrated here was probably used in rituals held to insure a successful hunt. Mask-making in the Eskimo world is most highly developed in southwestern Alaska and occurs only sporadically elsewhere.

Living Traditions: The Eskimo Hunters of the Arctic   **189**

Wooden Mask, Southwestern Alaska. 9″ high, 5½″ wide. Lent by the American Museum of Natural History, New York. (6/259)

The Eskimo believe that in lonely places there are evil spirits which may bring misfortune and illness. The medicine men claim that they gain control over the spirits and keep them from doing harm.

This mask, representing one of these spirits, is trimmed with fur and feathers. The area around the closed eye is light pink with white spots. The rest of the face is white.

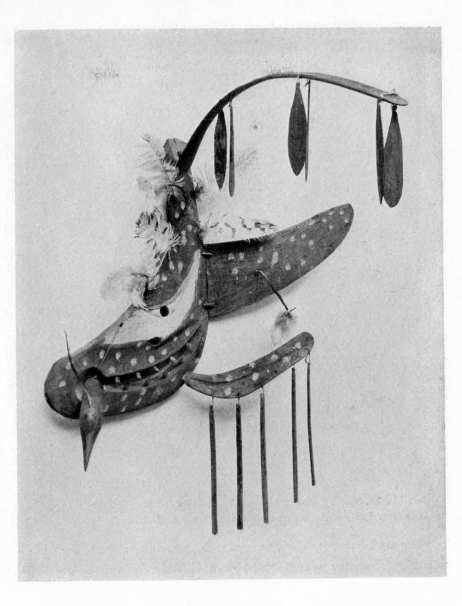

Wooden Mask, Southwestern Alaska. 22″ greatest dimension. Lent by the Museum of the American Indian, Heye Foundation, New York. (9/3409)

The mask represents a swan that drives white whales to the hunters in the spring. It is a fine example of the use of seemingly unrelated form elements, combined with extreme distortion of features. Both these characteristics appear frequently together in Eskimo masks made for magic purposes. Collected before 1919 by A. H. Twitchell on the Kuskokwin River.

Living Traditions: The Eskimo Hunters of the Arctic   **191**

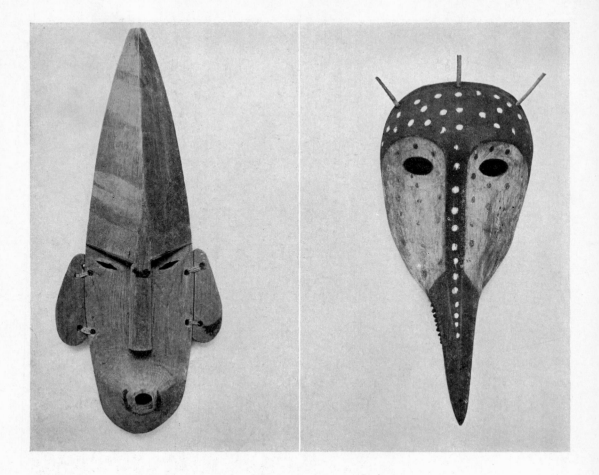

Wooden Masks, Southwestern Alaska. Left, 22¼″ long; right, 11¼″ long. Lent by the Museum of the American Indian, Heye Foundation, New York. (Left, 5/8667; right, 10/6031)

Left: The mask is meant to be a caricature of a person who lives in the "up river" backwoods and is therefore somewhat scorned by the more civilized "down river" people. It is possible that this severe type of carving was the basis on which the later elaborate masks were developed by the Eskimo under the influence of their Indian neighbors, the carvers of the Northwest Coast. Collected before 1917 by G. T. Emmons at Anvik.

Right: This mask represents an unidentified animal. It is typical of the simplification of organic forms reminiscent of some of the earliest Eskimo work. Color is used very sparingly on these masks and the grain of the wood shows even through the painted areas. Collected before 1921 at Anvik.

Near Anvik on the lower Yukon the coastal Eskimo meet the Indians of the interior. Both groups use masks and their work is almost indistinguishable.

Wooden Mask, Southwestern Alaska. 11¾″ overall diameter. Lent by the Museum of the American Indian, Heye Foundation, New York. (9/3425)

This mask is said to represent the spirit of autumn. Like the mask on page 191, it reflects an interest in the vague borderline between terror and laughter which is characteristic of Eskimo art and belief. The combination of these two elements appears again and again in Eskimo myths and rituals, and is probably consciously inserted by the artist into his work. Collected before 1919 by A. H. Twitchell on the Kuskokwim River.

Living Traditions: The Eskimo Hunters of the Arctic

Ivory Toy, St. Lawrence Island, Alaska. 2½″ high, 1½″ wide across hips. Lent by the Museum of the American Indian, Heye Foundation, New York. (13/3520)

During the winter, Eskimo men carve walrus ivory toys for their children. Besides dolls, they make more complex figures, like the wrestlers illustrated here, and sometimes create large sets of figures such as groups of dancers and spectators. The rivalry between Eskimo villages is often settled by wrestling matches between local champions. The wrestlers lock arms and endeavor to throw each other by sheer strength unaided by tripping. Collected before 1924 by A. E. Thompson at Kokuluk.

194   *Living Traditions: The Eskimo Hunters of the Arctic*

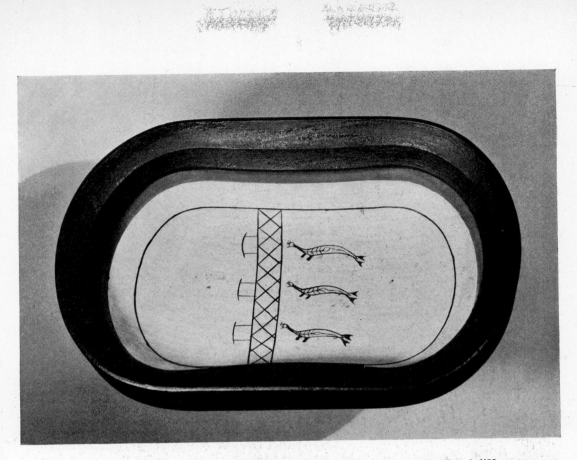

Wooden Bowl, Southwestern Alaska. 9¼″ long, 6¼″ wide, 2½″ deep. Lent by René d'Harnoncourt, Washington, D. C.

Because of the dense forests of the region, the Eskimo of southwestern Alaska use wood in their manufactures much more than the bands which inhabit the treeless northern coasts. Among these wooden objects are many dishes, buckets, trays and ladles. Practically identical vessels are made by the Indians who live inland just behind the Eskimo.

The simplest vessels are carved from single blocks of spruce wood. Dishes of the type illustrated here, however, have rims made as separate pieces and attached to the bases. To make these rims, thick strips of wood are made flexible by steaming and bent into shapes which fit on the edge of the blocks. The beveled ends of the strips overlap and are fastened together with wooden pegs or glue. The inner surface of the rim usually has a central ridge flanked by shallow grooves.

The bowls conventionally have the rims painted dark red and an unpainted base. The inside of the bottom is commonly decorated with fine black line drawings of animals, mythological beings or geometric figures. These drawings are closely related in spirit to the line engravings on ivory. Three seals are drawn in the bowl illustrated here. The red color is ocher or oxide of iron. The black is charcoal or gunpowder mixed with blood. Collected in 1939 by Virgil Farrell.

Living Traditions: The Eskimo Hunters of the Arctic   **195**

Wooden Hat, Southwestern Alaska. 8″ high, 13⅜″ long. Lent by the Museum of the American Indian, Heye Foundation, New York. (10/6921)

This hat is a very fine example of a kind of headgear worn by native hunters in southeastern Alaska and on the Aleutian Islands. The hunters pursue sea animals and birds in light skin kayaks which lie so low in the water that the glare from the water's surface disturbs the hunter's aim. To keep out the glare the visors of the hats are made very wide. Aleutian hats are more elaborately decorated than those of the Eskimo, for beside ivory ornaments of the type illustrated here, they have ornate painted designs and upstanding rows of sea lion whiskers.

These hats have developed from masks representing the creatures pursued by the hunters. Formerly if a man wished to hunt a seal, for example, he wore a mask representing that animal. By so doing he hoped to establish a friendly relationship with the animal, make it less fearful by appearing to be a seal himself and so attract it to him.

By a long process of cultural evolution the realistic masks lost their original character and became hats on which the faces of the animals still persisted in the form of decorations now so highly conventionalized as to be almost unrecognizable. Collected before 1921 on the Yukon River.

Living Traditions: The Eskimo Hunters of the Arctic

Indian Art for Modern Living

There are probably more craftsmen among Indians, proportionately, than among any other racial group in the United States. In almost every tribe crafts continue to fulfill either an economic or a spiritual need. Even the younger generation is familiar with the processes of handiwork and knows the satisfaction derived from shaping things with one's own hands.

It has often been said that Indian arts are on the decline because there is no place for them in the twentieth century. Many people think of Indian products as worthless knickknacks or as savage relics that belong in scientific collections or trophy rooms. It is true, of course, that the Indian craftsman, under the pressure of the white man's demand, produces many things merely for their souvenir value. It is also true that some of his traditional crafts are so specialized that they can be used only in their original environment. But the basic soundness and vigor of Indian art are constantly producing articles that reflect the strength of Indian traditions and fit perfectly into the contemporary scene. As a matter of fact, Indian art not only has a place but actually fills a concrete need in the United States today. Its close relationship to America, the land, and its unexplored wealth of forms offer a valuable contribution to modern American art and life.

Fig. 82. Navaho cast silver pins and bracelet, New Mexico. Lent by Mrs. Kenneth B. Disher and Mrs. René d'Harnoncourt. All pieces were made in 1938 or 1939.

Cherokee Wastepaper Basket, North Carolina. Lent anonymously.

Many contemporary tribal products can be used without adaptation in modern homes and as parts of modern dress. Among them are rugs, baskets, pottery, jewelry, toys, fur garments, moccasins, gloves, bags, belts and all kinds of embroideries and appliqué work. Some of these may find a place in our houses and wardrobes simply because of their decorative value, but many combine utility with aesthetic merit. Fine Navaho rugs, for instance, are among the most durable floor

198

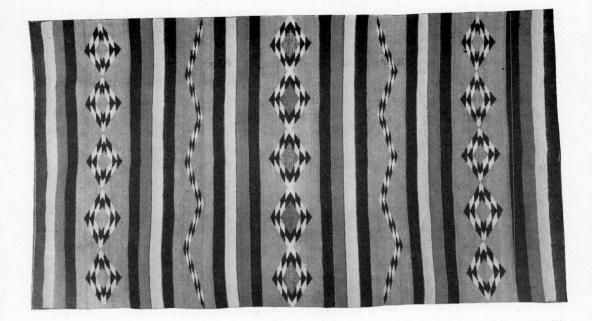

Fig. 84. Navaho floor rug, New Mexico. Lent by the Indian Arts and Crafts Board, United States Department of the Interior.

coverings that can be found; and Indian skin work, to choose one other example from many, compares favorably in quality, softness and strength with any similar product.

The current popular judgment of Indian handicrafts has unfortunately been based largely on the type of articles most often sold to tourists. In recent years, to meet the demands of the tourist trade in the United States and Alaska, new types of products with particularly "quaint" designs and riotous colors have been developed. Such articles actually reflect the customer's idea of Indian art rather than the taste of their maker. An Indian weaver who was once asked to give an opinion of a blanket with especially loud colors remarked, "It's too much white man's Indian for me."

Good Indian work, done without the interference of whites, includes restrained colors as well as bright ones, and usually leans to economy rather than complexity of design. It shows a

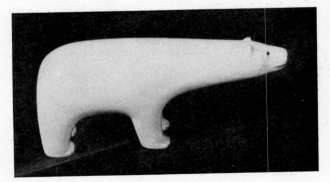

Fig. 85. Eskimo ivory toy, Alaska. Lent by the Indian Arts and Crafts Board, United States Department of the Interior.

careful balance of design and color, and so is neither restless nor confused. This subtle control of its elements and the close relationship between function and form are what bring Indian work so near to the aims of most contemporary artists and make it blend with any surroundings that are truly of the twentieth century.

Now, as always, tribal craftsmen are adapting products in their own way to fill new needs. This does not mean that their work must lose its identity. For hundreds of years this identity has persisted in every new form created by every new impulse of Indian life, and it will do so as long as there are Indian people. As their own lives change, with the introduction into their world of new means of transportation and other modern facilities, the scope of their experience grows and is reflected in a widening range of products. Especially interesting developments are occurring just now in the production of handwoven materials made by the bolt, and other handloomed articles. New types of products are also appearing in wood, silver, skin, pottery and many other mediums. Several new art forms have developed among various tribes in recent years that are closer to our own concepts of art and seek to replace functional values with aesthetic ones. The most prominent of these are the murals and water colors executed by Indian painters in New Mexico, Oklahoma and the Dakotas. These paintings retain much of the style and the feeling for proportion displayed in traditional tribal art and may well be the beginning of a new phase of Indian art. Examples are shown on pages 208, 209, 210.

The future of Indian crafts is, of course, bound to that of all handicrafts the world over and must be considered as part of this general picture. Under the ever increasing pressure of low-priced factory-made articles, the handicrafts have lost much of their market. At the same time it is evident that the factory can never entirely satisfy the needs of people who prefer individual designs and individual workmanship in some, at least, of their possessions. The present increase of public interest in the handicrafts indicates that this demand is rapidly growing, and that we are in a period of transition which will eventually lead to the establishment of two distinct markets, one for handicrafts and the other for factory products.

Whatever the eventual outcome, we know for certain that fine Indian arts and crafts can safely develop for many years, since most of their potential market has not even been touched. We also know that the Indian artist, due to his traditions, manual ability, patience and modest demands, can easily compete with other contemporary craftsmen.

To develop fully the potential market for Indian work and to organize production to meet the requirements of modern merchandising will, of course, be a slow and delicate process. But the moral and economic benefits it could yield to the Indian producer and the enrichment it would mean for our own world, make it a task that is one of the responsibilities of America today.

Navaho Silverwork from Arizona and New Mexico.

The most striking evidence of the affinity between traditional Indian art and modern art forms can be seen in Navaho silverwork. While many pieces, like the silver cup shown here, are made exclusively for the white man's use, their designs retain all the fundamental characteristics of the traditional tribal style.

Indian Art for Modern Living

Two Seminole Dolls from Florida and a Woven Papago Toy from Southern Arizona.

Almost every tribe in the United States and Alaska made dolls and toys for its children. The Seminole dolls shown here are made of coconut fiber and dressed in miniature replicas of the traditional tribal costume. The Papago bird is woven from leaves.

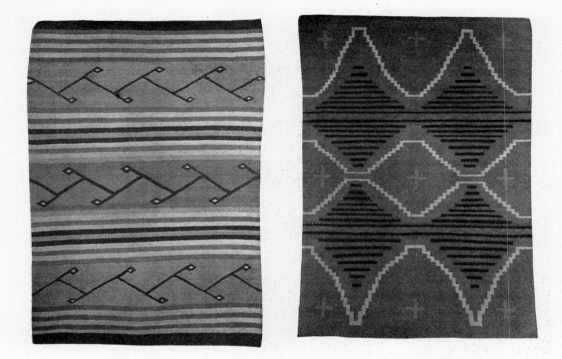

Modern Navaho Rugs from Arizona. Lent by the United States Office of Indian Affairs.

The recent revival of interest among Navaho weavers in the use of vegetable dyes and old blanket patterns produced a new type of rug that shows how traditional tribal designs blend with contemporary styles of decoration. The rug on the left is dyed entirely with soft vegetable colors. Its design is reminiscent of the striped blankets of an early period, while the rug on the right illustrates a revival of the terraced patterns of the classic period.

Indian Art for Modern Living

Pottery Platter from San Ildefonso Pueblo, New Mexico; Papago Pottery Jar from Southern Arizona.

Indian pottery from the Southwest is best known for its intricately painted design but in many instances its outstanding merit consists in simplicity of shape and exquisite surface treatment.

204   *Indian Art for Modern Living*

Hopi Shawl from Arizona. Lent by the Indian Arts and Crafts Board, United States Department of the Interior.

This brown and white Hopi shawl is a typical example of the simple patterns and conservative colors so often found in traditional Indian crafts. Shawls, like all Hopi textiles, are woven by men.

Indian Art for Modern Living

Osage Beaded and Braided Belt from Oklahoma, used as trimming on a short evening cape.

The combination of beadwork and braiding is often found among the tribes now living in central and northern Oklahoma. The belt is divided on both ends into narrow tasseled strips that are here seen hanging from the yoke. The cape was designed by F. A. Picard for the Indian Arts and Crafts Board.

Seminole Cotton Patchwork from Florida, applied to an after-skiing suit.

The Florida Seminole developed elaborate costumes from fabrics made of narrow strips of colored cotton goods. In many cases these strips are in turn sewed together in many small rectangles and triangles, but in the blouses of the older people the original simple stripes have survived. The bodice of this suit, designed by F. A. Picard for the Indian Arts and Crafts Board, is made from such a blouse. The buttons are Navaho hammered silver.

Indian Art for Modern Living

The Delight Makers, a Gouache by Fred Kabotie, Hopi. Lent by Charles de Young Elkus, San Francisco.

Fred Kabotie was one of the first Hopi artists to produce easel paintings. The ceremonial dances of his tribe constitute his favorite subject matter. He is deeply interested in tribal tradition and reproduces all details of costumes and ceremonial paraphernalia with painstaking care.

Kabotie is now employed by the United States Bureau of Indian Affairs as a teacher of painting at the Hopi high school at Oraibi, Arizona, and supervised the making of the reproductions of ancient murals from Awatovi and Kawaika-a shown on pages 23, 111 and 112.

Indian Art for Modern Living

Plains Indian on Horseback, a Gouache by Oscar Howe, Sioux. Lent by Margaretta S. Dietrich, Santa Fé, New Mexico.

The tradition of representative painting was more fully developed among the Plains tribes than among any other group in the United States. At any rate skin garments from the eighteenth century decorated with pictorial records of battles are still in existence. In the nineteenth century these records became more realistic and more elaborate and were widely used for the decoration of skin robes and canvas sheets issued to the Indians by the Army.

Drawings in colored crayons made by Indian prisoners of war for Army officers are also frequently found. Modern Plains painting still preserves the strong feeling of motion and the delicacy typical of their traditional art.

Indian Art for Modern Living

Bird in Flight, a Gouache by Munroe Tsa-to-ke, Kiowa. Lent by Mrs. William Denman, San Francisco.

Navaho Weaver, a Gouache by Harrison Begay, Navaho. Lent by Mrs. Walter Rullman, New York.

Indian Art for Modern Living

Bibliography

This brief bibliography is divided into sections corresponding with those in the book. Within each section the entries are arranged alphabetically by authors wherever possible. The first four sections are concerned with the general matters dealt with in the introduction to the book. The remaining sections cover the regional aspects of Indian art, and their backgrounds, which are discussed in the prehistoric and historic chapters of the book.

The bibliography has been selected from an enormous number of works about Indians. The references in each section have been chosen from two points of view: basic scientific importance and concern with art. In addition certain popular works and books for children have been included because of their well-rounded and illustrated descriptions of native life. With a very few exceptions all references are illustrated.

The bibliographical form is modelled upon that used by the *Art Index*.

Sample entry: Mallery, Garrick. Picture writing of the American Indians. BAE-R 10:1–777 1889.

Explanation: An article by Garrick Mallery, entitled "Picture Writing of the American Indians," will be found in the Bureau of American Ethnology Report for the year 1889, volume 10, pages 1 to 777, inclusive.

Abbreviations

I. NAMES OF INSTITUTIONS AND PUBLICATIONS ISSUED BY THEM:

AAA-M   American Anthropological Association, Memoirs. Menasha, Wisconsin

AAns   American Anthropological Association, American Anthropologist, new series. Menasha, Wisconsin

AFS-M   American Folk-Lore Society, Memoirs. New York

AMNH-AP American Museum of Natural History, Anthropological Papers. New York

AMNH-B   American Museum of Natural History, Bulletins. New York

AMNH-H   American Museum of Natural History, Handbook. New York

AMNH-M   American Museum of Natural History, Memoirs. New York

ANSP-J   Academy of Natural Sciences of Philadelphia, Journal. Philadelphia

APS-M   American Philosophical Society, Memoirs. Philadelphia

APS-P   American Philosophical Society, Proceedings. Philadelphia

BAE-B   Bureau of American Ethnology, Bulletins. Washington

BAE-R   Bureau of American Ethnology, Reports. Washington

CIW-P   Carnegie Institution of Washington, Publications. Washington

CU-CA   Columbia University, Contributions to Anthropology. New York

DAM-L   Denver Art Museum, Leaflets. Denver, Colorado

FM-AS   Field Museum of Natural History, Anthropological Series. Chicago

GP-MP   Gila Pueblo, Medallion Papers. Globe, Arizona

LA-B   Laboratory of Anthropology, Bulletins. Santa Fe, New Mexico

LA-M   Laboratory of Anthropology, Memoirs. Santa Fe, New Mexico

LGS-AS   Louisiana Geological Survey, Anthropological Studies. New Orleans, Louisiana.

MAI-C   Museum of the American Indian, Heye Foundation, Contributions. New York

MAI-INM Museum of the American Indian, Heye Foundation, Indian Notes and Monographs. New York

MNA-B   Museum of Northern Arizona, Bulletins. Flagstaff, Arizona

MPM-B   Milwaukee Public Museum, Bulletins. Milwaukee, Wisconsin

NGS   National Geographic Society, Washington

NMC-B   National Museum of Canada, Bulletins. Ottawa

NMC-M   National Museum of Canada, Memoirs. Ottawa

PM-P   Peabody Museum, Papers. Cambridge, Massachusetts

SI-AR   Smithsonian Institution, Annual Reports. Washington

SI-MC   Smithsonian Institution, Miscellaneous Collections. Washington

SM-P   Southwest Museum, Papers. Los Angeles, California

UC-PA   University of Chicago, Publications in Anthropology. Chicago

UCPAAE   University of California, Publications in American Archaeology and Ethnology. Berkeley, California

UP-MJ   University of Pennsylvania, Museum Journal. Philadelphia

USNM-AR United States National Museum, Annual Reports. Washington

Abbreviations (Cont'd)

USNM-P United States National Museum, Proceedings. Washington
UW-PA University of Washington, Publications in Anthropology. Seattle, Washington

Selected Bibliography

FUNDAMENTAL PUBLICATIONS FOR THE STUDY OF THE INDIAN RACE NORTH OF MEXICO

Curtis, E. S. The North American Indian. 30 v. Cambridge, 1903–30. *Descriptions of most existing tribes. Each volume is accompanied by a portfolio of large photographs.*

Douglas, Frederic H. A guidebook to articles on Indians. 280 p. mimeographed. Denver Art Museum, 1934. *Listings of articles in about 150 scientific serials.*

——— ed. The Indian leaflet series. Denver Art Museum, 1930–date. *100 leaflets dealing with many phases of Indian life. Referred to individually below as DAM-L.*

Essays in historical anthropology of North America. Published in honor of John R. Swanton. 600 p. SI-MC 100 1940. *Full, up-to-date discussions of physical types, ancient man, southeastern, basin, plains and Eskimo archaeology, early Navaho, Athapaskan and Iroquois history.*

Harding, Anne, and Bolling, Patricia. Bibliography of articles and papers on North American Indian art. 365 p. mimeographed. Washington, Department of the Interior, Indian Arts and Crafts Board, 1938. *The best available bibliography of Indian art.*

Hodge, Frederick W., ed. Handbook of the American Indians north of Mexico. 2 v. 1221 p. BAE-B 30 1907–10. *The standard encyclopedia on the Indian.*

Holling, Holling C. The book of Indians. 125 p. N. Y., Platt and Munk, 1935. *Primarily for children but valuable for its many careful drawings of crafts.*

Jenness, Diamond, ed. The American aborigines: their origin and antiquity. 396 p. Toronto, Univ. of Toronto Press, 1933. *Papers by ten scientists dealing with Indian origins, history and culture.*

——— The Indians of Canada. 429 p. NMC-B 65 1934. *A general handbook on the subject.*

Kroeber, Alfred L. Cultural and natural areas of native North America. 242 p. UCPAAE 38 1939. *The most detailed study of Indian population and culture as related to environment.*

Sapir, Edward. Central and North American languages. Encyclopedia Britannica, 14th ed. 5:138–141 1932. *A good summary about Indian language groupings and characteristics.*

Sauer, Carl. Man and nature. 273 p. N. Y., Scribners,
1939. *Indian life as seen by the human geographer. Though written for children, the book is of great interest to adults.*

Vaillant, George C., Lothrop, S. K. et al., eds. The Maya and their neighbors. 606 p. N. Y., Appleton Century, 1940. *Contains authoritative articles by a number of scientists. Important for up-to-date discussions of several phases of United States archaeology; and of relationships of United States and Mexican Indians.*

Wissler, Clark. The American Indian. 3d ed. 466 p. N. Y., Oxford Univ. Press, 1938. *The only general book on the subject. Includes Central and South America.*

——— Indians of the United States; four centuries of their history and culture. 319 p. Garden City, Doubleday, Doran, 1940. *The best popular description of the tribes.*

INDIAN ORIGINS AND EARLY HISTORY

Bryan, Kirk, and Ray, Louis L. Geologic antiquity of the Lindenmeier site in Colorado. 76 p. SI-MC 99: no. 2 1940. *The latest statement about this important Pleistocene site, 15 to 20 thousand years old.*

Campbell, Elizabeth, and Campbell, W. C. An archaeological survey of the Twenty-nine Palms Region. 91 p. SM-P 7 1931. *Describes one of the very ancient sites in the far west.*

Harrington, Mark R. Gypsum Cave, Nevada. 197 p. SM-P 8 1933. *A full description of a site occupied some 8000 years ago.*

Hooton, E. A. Up from the ape. 626 p. N. Y., MacMillan, 1931. *A clear description of Indian physical types.*

Howard, E. B. Evidence of early man in America. UP-MJ 24:61–175 1935. *A summary of the evidence available at the time.*

Jenks, Albert E. Minnesota's Brown's Valley man and associated burial artifacts. 49 p. AAA-M 49 1937. *A possible Pleistocene burial described and discussed.*

MacCurdy, G. G., ed. Early man, as depicted by leading authorities at the International Symposium, Academy of Natural Sciences, Philadelphia, March, 1937. 362 p. Philadelphia, Lippincott, 1937.

Sauer, Carl. American agricultural origins. In: Essays in anthropology, presented to A. L. Kroeber in celebration of his sixtieth birthday. p. 279–297. Berkeley, Univ. of California Press, 1936. *A recent discussion of this important subject.*

Strong, William Duncan. Introduction to Nebraska archeology. 315 p. SI-MC 93:no. 10, 1935. *Important here for its description of the Signal Butte site, tentatively dated as 2000 to 4000 years old.*

INDIAN ART

Alexander, H. B. Pueblo Indian painting. Folio, 18 p. 50 il. Nice, France, C. Szwedzicki, 1932. *A portfolio of color reproductions of water colors.*

Boas, Franz. Primitive art. 376 p. Cambridge, Harvard Univ. Press, 1927. *The only full-length book on the subject; not restricted to Indian art, though about half is devoted to the best discussion of Northwest Coast art.*

Exposition of Indian tribal arts, Inc., N. Y. Introduction to American Indian art, I. 57 p. 1931. *Text by John Sloan and Oliver La Farge. An appraisal of Indian art in its various manifestations.*

———— Introduction to American Indian art, II. 81 p. 1931. CONTENTS: *H. J. Spinden, Fine art and the first Americans, Indian symbolism; Mary Austin, Indian pottery; Alice C. Henderson, Modern Indian painting; Laura A. Armer, Sandpainting of the Navajo Indians; Frances L. Newcombe, Description of sandpainting; K. M. Chapman, Indian pottery; N. M. Judd, Indian sculpture and carving; C. C. Willoughby, Indian masks; E. W. Gifford, Indian basketry; Mary L. Kissell, Indian weaving; W. C. Orchard, Indian porcupine quill and bead work; Ruth Gaines, Books on Indian arts north of Mexico.*

Jacobson, O. B. Kiowa Indian art. Folio, 11 p. 30 il. Nice, France, C. Szwedzicki, 1929. *Color reproductions of water colors.*

Linton, Ralph C. Primitive art. Kenyon Review 3:34–51 Jan. 1941. *An illuminating discussion of the "primitive" in native arts.*

Sides, Dorothy. Decorative art of the southwestern Indians. Folio with 50 il. Santa Ana, Calif., Fine Arts Press, 1936.

Vaillant, George C. Indian arts in North America. 63 p. N. Y., Harpers, 1939. *A detailed analysis of Indian art, with 96 full-page plates.*

MAJOR TECHNIQUES OF INDIAN ART

Technical references not listed in this section should be sought in the regional sections of this bibliography.

Douglas, Frederic H. Basketry construction technics. 3 p. DAM-L 67 1935.

———— Basketry decoration technics. 3 p. DAM-L 68 1935

———— Indian cloth-making; looms, technics and kinds of fabrics. 7 p. DAM-L 59–60 1933.

———— Indian basketry, varieties and distribution. 3 p. DAM-L 58 1933.

Holmes, William H. Art in shell of the ancient Americans. BAE-R 2:176–305 1881.

———— Form and ornament in ceramic art. BAE-R 4:437–465 1883. *An extremely important study.*

———— Handbook of aboriginal American antiquities 380 p. BAE-B 60 1919. *The best source on Indian stone tool and weapon making.*

Jeancon, Jean Allard and Douglas, Frederic H. Indian sandpainting; tribes, techniques and uses. 7 p. DAM-L 43–44 1932.

Mason, Otis T. Aboriginal American basketry. USNM-AR 1902:185–545. *The classic work on the subject.*

Orchard, William C. The technique of porcupine-quill decoration among the North American Indians. 53 p. MAI-C 4 1916. *Important for technical details.*

———— Beads and beadwork of the American Indians. 140 p. MAI-C 11 1929. *A very detailed description of the craft.*

Weltfish, Gene. Prehistoric North American basketry, techniques and modern distributions. AAns 32:454–495 1930. *The most important modern survey.*

THE CARVERS OF THE FAR WEST

Heye, George G. Certain artifacts from San Miguel Island, California. 211 p. MAI-INM 7:no 4 1921. *Contains a résumé of the region's history.*

Preble, Donna. Yamino-Kwiti; boy runner of Siba. 236 p. Caldwell, Idaho, Caxton Press, 1940. *A children's story but full of much accurate information and well illustrated with careful drawings.*

Rogers, David B. Prehistoric man of the Santa Barbara coast. 452 p. Santa Barbara Museum of Natural History, 1929. *An important study of the Santa Barbara region tribes.*

THE CARVERS OF THE NORTHWEST COAST

De Laguna, Frederica. The archaeology of Cook Inlet, Alaska. 263 p. Phila., Univ. of Pennsylvania Press, 1934. *This detailed study deals primarily with Eskimo material but touches on the archaeology of the extreme northern Northwest Coast.*

Smith, Harlan I. An album of prehistoric Canadian art. 195 p. NMC-B 37 1923. *Contains illustrations of a number of Northwest Coast carvings.*

THE ENGRAVERS OF THE ARCTIC

Collins, Henry B. Prehistoric art of the Alaskan Eskimo. 52 p. SI-MC 81:no. 14 1929. *A description of the Old Bering Sea style and its successors.*

De Laguna, Frederica. The archaeology of Cook Inlet, Alaska. 263 p. Phila., Univ. of Pennsylvania Press, 1934. *Sites in Southern Alaska and the finds from them fully discussed.*

Jochelson, Vladimir I. Archeological investigations in the Aleutian Islands. 145 p. CIW-P 367 1925.

Mason, J. Alden. Eskimo pictorial art. UP-MJ 18:248–283 1927. *Modern ivory engraving described.*

Selected Bibliography (Cont'd)

THE SCULPTORS OF THE EAST

Bolton, Reginald Pelham. Indian life of long ago in the city of New York. 167 p. N. Y., Graham, 1934. *A popular description with many excellent drawings.*

Bushnell, David I., Jr. Native villages and village sites east of the Mississippi. 111 p. BAE-B 69 1919. *Descriptions largely based on eyewitness reports.*

Cushing, Frank H. Exploration of ancient key dwellers' remains on the Gulf Coast of Florida. APS-P 35:329–432 1896. *A description of the rich Key Marco site.*

Douglas, Frederic H. Copper and the Indian. 7 p. DAM-L 75–76 1936. *Summary of the available information.*

Ford, James A. Analyses of Indian village site collections from Louisiana and Mississippi. 285 p. LGS-AS 2 1936. *Studies in the development of some typical prehistoric southern design styles.*

———— and Willey, Gordon. Crooks site; a Marksville period burial mound in . . . Louisiana. 148 p. LGS-AS 3 1940. *Valuable for its indications of the early history of the Hopewell culture.*

Holmes, William H. Aboriginal pottery of the eastern United States. 201 p. BAE-R 20 1899. *The standard work on the subject.*

Moore, Clarence B. Articles on aboriginal sites in the Southeast. ANSP-J 10–16 1894–1918. *Descriptions of hundreds of sites and specimens; an extremely important work for anthropologists and artists.*

Moorehead, Warren K., ed. Etowah papers. 178 p. Andover, Mass., Phillips Academy; New Haven, Yale Univ. Press, 1932. *Includes papers by C. C. Willoughby on Moundbuilder art; Zelia Nuttall on the question of Mexican influence on United States Indians.*

Rochester Museum of Arts and Sciences. Research records. 1926–date. *An important series dealing with the archaeology of New York.*

Shetrone, H. C. The mound builders. 508 p. N. Y., Appleton, 1930. *The only work dealing with the subject as a whole.*

Vaillant, George C. Some resemblances in the ceramics of Central and Northern America. 37 p. GP-MP 12 1932. *An important study of specific details of the relationship between the Indians north and south of the Mexican border.*

Willoughby, Charles C. Antiquities of the New England Indians. 314 p. Cambridge, Peabody Museum, Harvard Univ., 1935. *The standard work on New England archaeology.*

———— The art of the great earthwork builders of Ohio. In: Holmes Anniversary Volume. p. 469–480, Washington, James W. Bryan Press, 1916. *Illustrates and comments on many of the great pieces of Moundbuilder art.*

THE PAINTERS OF THE SOUTHWEST

Amsden, Charles A. An analysis of Hohokam pottery designs. 54 p. GP-MP 23 1936. *A discussion of the development and relative frequency of various design elements.*

Bandelier, Adolph. The delight-makers. 490 p. N. Y., Dodd-Mead, 1916. *A novel of prehistoric Pueblo life.*

Cosgrove, H. S., and C. B. The Swarts ruin; a typical Mimbres site in southwest New Mexico. 170 p. PM-P 15 1932. *This report contains a very large number of drawings of Mimbres pottery designs.*

Douglass, Andrew E. Dating Pueblo Bonito and other ruins of the Southwest. 74 p. NGS Contributed technical papers, Pueblo Bonito series 1, Washington, 1935. *A full account of the tree ring calendar by its discoverer.*

Gladwin, Harold S. et al. Excavations at Snaketown. Material culture. 305 p. Comparisons and theories. 167 p. GP-MP 25 & 26, 1937. *The fullest report on a Hohokam site. Paper 26 is important for its bold hypotheses concerning man in the Americas.*

Medallion Papers, Globe, Arizona, Gila Pueblo, 1928–date. *The most important series dealing with the Hohokam and Pueblo cultures of the southern Southwest—referred to here individually as GP-MP.*

Mera, H. P. Ceramic clues to the prehistory of north central New Mexico. 43 p. LA-B technical series 8 1935. *The early history of the region traced through its pottery.*

Morris, Ann A. Digging in the Southwest. 301 p. Garden City, N. Y., Doubleday, Doran, 1933. *A good popular account of southwestern archaeology.*

Morris, Earl H. Archeological studies in the La Plata district. 298 p. CIW-P 519 1939. *A very sound and full analysis of Pueblo archaeology.*

Papers of the Southwest Expedition. Andover, Mass., Phillips Academy; New Haven, Yale Univ. Press, 1924. *This series deals with the excavation of Pecos ruin and is one of the most important in the field of southwestern archaeology. There are a number of large volumes, some of which deal with related modern subjects.*

Roberts, Frank H. H., Jr. A survey of southwestern archeology. SI-AR 1935:507–533. *Outlines the characteristics and sequence of prehistoric periods.*

PICTOGRAPHS

Mallery, Garrick. Picture writing of the American Indians. BAE-R 10:1–777 1889. *The most important single work on pictographs.*

Steward, Julian H. Petroglyphs of California and adjoining states. UCPAAE 24:47–238 1929. *A thorough going analysis of the distribution of design elements occurring in pictographs of the West.*

—— Petroglyphs of the United States. SI-AR 1936: 405–426. *The most recent general survey of the subject.*

THE PUEBLO CORNPLANTERS

Bunzel, Ruth. The Pueblo potter. 134 p. CU-CA 8 1929. *A careful study of the various aspects of pottery decoration.*

Chapman, Kenneth M. The pottery of Santo Domingo pueblo; a detailed study of its decoration. 192 p. LA-M 1 1939. *The most complete study of the pottery designs of one pueblo.*

—— Pueblo Indian pottery. 2 v. 100 plates. Nice, France, C. Szwedzicki, 1933 and 1936. *Portfolios of large color plates of important pottery types.*

Douglas, Frederic H. Main types of Pueblo wool textiles. 7 p. DAM-L 94–95 1940. *Detailed descriptions.*

—— Main types of Pueblo cotton textiles. 7 p. DAM-L 92–93 1940. *Detailed descriptions.*

—— Modern Pueblo pottery types. 7 p. DAM-L 53–54 1933. *Detailed descriptions.*

—— Modern Pueblo Indian villages. 7 p. DAM-L 45–46 1937. *History, names, population and main fiesta dates.*

Goddard, Pliny E. Indians of the Southwest. 196 p. AMNH-H 2 1931. *The best popular summary of the subject.*

Guthe, Carl E. Pueblo pottery making. 89 p. Papers of the Southwest expedition, 2. Andover, Mass. Phillips Academy; New Haven, Yale Univ. Press, 1925. *An exhaustive study of pottery making technique at San Ildefonso pueblo.*

Kennard, Edward A. Hopi kachinas. 40 p. N. Y., Augustin, 1938. *The best modern study of the subject with 28 color plates of paintings by Ferdinand Pinney Earle.*

Kubler, George. The religious architecture of New Mexico. 232 p. Colorado Springs, Taylor Museum, 1940. *A very important detailed study of a previously neglected subject. Included here because this architecture was influenced by that of the Pueblo Indians.*

Mera, H. P. The "Rain Bird"; a study in pueblo design. 113 p. LA-M 2 1937. *This monograph follows a single element in Pueblo pottery design through 1500 years of its history.*

—— Style trends of Pueblo pottery in the Rio Grande and Little Colorado cultural areas from the 16th to the 19th centuries. 164 p. LA-M 3 1939. *The only available book on the pottery of this period.*

Museum of Northern Arizona publications. Flagstaff, Arizona. Museum notes (1928–1938), Bulletin (1932–date), Plateau (1938–date). *These serials contain important information on many phases of southwestern archaeology and ethnology.*

Parsons, Elsie Clews, ed. The Hopi journal of Alexander M. Stephen. 2 v. 1417 p. CU-CA 23 1936. *A primary source of information on the Hopi, with many comparative notes.*

—— Pueblo religion. 2 v. 1275 p. UC-PA 1939. *A comparative, descriptive analysis that touches most phases of Pueblo life.*

Stevenson, Matilda C. The Zuni Indians. 634 p. BAE-R 23 1902. *The classic study of this pueblo, with an immense body of detailed information.*

Underhill, Ruth M. First penthouse dwellers of America. 155 p. N. Y., Augustin, 1938. *An attractive popular account of the Pueblo Indians.*

THE NAVAHO SHEPHERDS

Amsden, Charles. Navaho weaving; its technique and history. 261 p. Santa Ana, Calif., The Fine Arts Press, 1934. *The best available work on Navaho weaving history.*

Bedinger, Margery. Navajo Indian silverwork. 43 p. The Old West series 8. Denver, John Van Male, 1936. *Especially valuable for its information on techniques.*

Coolidge, Dane, and Mary Roberts. The Navajo Indians. 316 p. N. Y., Houghton Mifflin, 1930. *Despite its too great dependency on certain informants, this is an excellent study of the tribe.*

Franciscan Fathers. An ethnological dictionary of the Navaho language. 536 p. St. Michael's, Arizona, 1910. *The best source of information on the tribe.*

Left-handed. Son of Old Man Hat, recorded by Walter Dyk. 378 p. N. Y., Harcourt, Brace, 1938. *A Navaho autobiography filled with important data on tribal life and customs.*

Matthews, Washington. Navaho legends. 299 p. AFS-M 5 1897. *The first important study of the Navaho.*

Mera, H. P. Papers on Navaho blanket types. LA-B general series. 1938–date. *Brief studies of types; contains information not found elsewhere.*

Reichard, Gladys. Navajo shepherd and weaver. 222 p. N. Y., Augustin, 1936. *The best description of modern Navaho weaving technique.*

—— and Newcomb, Franc J. Shooting chant; sandpaintings of the Navajo. 87 p. N. Y., Augustin, 1937. *A complete description by modern authorities of a Navaho ceremony with many color plates of sand paintings.*

Woodward, Arthur. A brief history of Navaho silver-smithing. 78 p. MNA-B 14 1938. *The standard work on the subject and the only source of many details.*

THE APACHE MOUNTAIN PEOPLE

Douglas, Frederic H. Apache basketry 3 p. DAM-L 64 1934. *Description of all types.*

Goodwin, Grenville. The social divisions and economic life of the western Apache. AANS 37:55–64 1935. *One of the few careful studies of these people.*

———— Myths and tales of the White Mountain Apache. 223 p. AFS-M 23 1939. *The White Mountain people are the Western Apache of Arizona.*

Hoijer, Harry. Chiricahua and Mescalero Apache texts; with ethnological notes by E. M. Opler. 219 p. UC-PA 1938. *The Apache of southern New Mexico and Arizona are described.*

Roberts, Helen H. The basketry of the San Carlos Apache. AMNH-AP 31:121–218 1929. *A detailed description of Western Apache basketry.*

THE DESERT DWELLERS OF THE SOUTHWEST

Beals, Ralph L. Material culture of the Pima, Papago and Western Apache. 44 p. Berkeley, Calif., U. S. Dept. of Int., National Park Service, 1934. *A very convenient compilation of scattered data.*

Forde, C. Daryll. Yuma ethnography. UCPAAE 28:83–278 1931. *Description of a typical Colorado River tribe.*

Gifford, E. W. Northeastern and western Yavapai. UCPAAE 34:247–354 1936. *The best available description of the tribe, often known as the Mohave-Apache or Yuma-Apache.*

Kroeber, Alfred L., ed. Walapai ethnography. 293 p. AAA-M 42 1935. *A detailed description of the tribe by various students.*

Russell, Frank. The Pima Indians. 390 p. BAE-R 26 1908. *A full description of the tribe. Much of it applies to the Papago also.*

Spier, Leslie. Havasupai ethnography. AMNH-AP 29:79–380 1929. *The details of tribal culture are described and supplemented by many comparative notes.*

———— Yuman tribes of the Gila river. 433 p. UC-PA 1933. *Deals principally with the Maricopa but gives many details about other little known Yuman tribes.*

Underhill, Ruth M. Singing for power; the song magic of the Papago Indians of southern Arizona. 158 p. Berkeley, Univ. of Calif. Press, 1938. *A study of the tribe's religion and ceremonies.*

THE SEED GATHERERS OF THE FAR WEST

Dixon, Roland B. Basketry designs of the Indians of northern California. AMNH-B 17:1–32 1902.

Kelly, Isabel T. The carver's art of the Indians of northwestern California. UCPAAE 24:343–360 1930.

Kroeber, Alfred L. Basket designs of the Mission Indians of California. AMNH-AP 20:149–185 1922.

———— Handbook of the Indians of California. 995 p. BAE-B 78 1925. *An encyclopedic treatment of the subject and the chief source of information about it.*

Publications in American archeology and ethnology. Berkeley, Univ. of Calif. Press, 1909–date. *A long series of scientific publications by various authors on most phases of California and Nevada Indian life. Here referred to individually as* UCPAAE.

THE HUNTERS OF THE PLAINS

American Museum of Natural History, N. Y. Anthropological papers. 1908–date. *Contains many studies of most of the Plains tribes. Here referred to as* AMNH-AP.

Douglas, Frederic H. Parfleches and other rawhide articles. 7 p. DAM-L 77–78 1936. *Notes on forms, techniques and designs.*

———— Plains beads and beadwork designs. 7 p. DAM-L 73–74 1936. *Notes on history and major design styles.*

Ewers, John C. Plains Indian painting. 84 p. Palo Alto, Calif., Stanford Univ. Press, 1939. *The first and only description of Plains painting on skin.*

Field Museum of Natural History, Chicago. Anthropological series, 1895–date. *Contains a large number of important papers on the Plains tribes, especially Cheyenne and Arapaho. Here referred to as* FM-AS.

Fletcher, Alice, and La Flesche, Francis. The Omaha tribe. 654 p. BAE-R 27, 1906. *Full-length description of a typical southeastern Plains tribe in which Plains and Woodland traits are mingled.*

Grinnell, George Bird. The Cheyenne Indians; their history and ways of life. 2 v. 788 p. New Haven, Yale Univ. Press, 1923. *The culture of a typical central Plains tribe.*

Hyde, George E. Red Cloud's folk; a history of the Oglala Sioux. 331 p. Norman, Univ. of Oklahoma Press, 1937. *Brings out clearly the briefness of Indian life on the plains in its most characteristic form.*

Kroeber, Alfred L. The Arapaho. AMNH-B 18:1–229, 279–454 1902. *Especially valuable for its analysis of Plains Indian crafts and design styles.*

Kurz, Friederich. Journal of life on the upper Missouri between 1846 and 1857. Ed. by J. N. B. Hewitt. 382 p. BAE-B 115 1937. *Contains all of the careful drawings by this German artist of Plains Indians and the details of their culture.*

Lowie, Robert H. The Crow Indians. 350 p. N. Y., Farrar & Rinehart, 1935. *A good description of northern Plains Indian life and how it works.*

Lyford, Carrie A. Quill and bead work of the western Sioux. 116 p. Washington, U. S. Office of Indian Affairs, 1940. *Contains much information on techniques and design styles not available elsewhere.*

Maximilian, Prince of Wied. Atlas of 81 paintings by Charles Bodmer. Early Western Travels series, v. 25. Cleveland, Clark, 1906. *Bodmer's paintings are the best pictorial source of information on the Plains Indians of the early 19th century.*

Wissler, Clark. North American Indians of the plains. 147 p. AMNH-H 1 1912. *The best popular guide to the subject.*

THE WOODSMEN OF THE EAST

De Bry, Theodor. Collectiones peregrinationum in Indiam orientalem et Indiam occidentalem. 37 v. Frankfort am Main, 1590–1634. *Contains dozens of engravings of eye witness drawings of 16th and 17th century eastern Indians.*

Densmore, Frances. Chippewa customs. 204 p. BAE-B 86 1929. *A full description of the life of a typical Great Lakes tribe.*

Harrington, M. R. Dickon among the Lenape Indians. 353 p. N. Y., Winston, 1938. *A story for boys, but of great value for its scientific accuracy and many detailed drawings.*

Hunt, George T. The wars of the Iroquois. 209 p. Madison, Univ. of Wisconsin Press, 1940. *The effect of the fur trade on the Iroquois and other northeastern tribes. An important modern study with much new data.*

Keesing, F. M. The Menomini Indians of Wisconsin. 261 p. APS-M 10 1939. *Follows the tribe through three centuries and shows how its life was affected by circumstances.*

Kenton, Edna, ed. The Indians of North America; from the Jesuit relations and allied documents. 2 v. 1179 p. N. Y., Harcourt, Brace, 1927. *Quotations from early accounts of the eastern tribes.*

MacCauley, Clay. The Seminole Indians of Florida. BAE-R 5:469–531 1888. *The first scientific account of the tribe which remains much the same today.*

Morgan, Lewis H. The league of the Iroquois. Ed. by Herbert M. Lloyd. 332 p. N. Y., Dodd-Mead, 1922. *The classic account of the tribe.*

Speck, Frank G. The double curve motive in northeastern Algonkian art. 17 p. NMC-M 42 1914. *The basic study of this important Indian design style.*

—— Decorative art and basketry of the Cherokee. MPM-B 2:53–86 1920. *Modern crafts and designs of southern Indians.*

—— Naskapi, the savage hunters of the Labrador peninsula. 248 p. Norman, Univ. of Oklahoma Press, 1935. *Description of a northern woodland tribe.*

—— Montagnais art in birchbark; a circumpolar trait. 157 p. MAI-INM 7: no. 2 1937. *The most important craft of the northeastern woodland tribes, with a full discussion of the floral art appearing on birchbark objects.*

—— Penobscot man; the life history of a forest tribe in Maine. 325 p. Phila., Univ. of Pennsylvania Press, 1940. *The only modern account of a typical New England tribe.*

Swanton, John R. Indian tribes of the lower Mississippi valley and adjacent coast of the Gulf of Mexico. 387 p. BAE-B 43 1911. *The standard work on the southeastern Indians as a whole.*

—— Final report of the De Soto expedition commission. 400 p. Washington, House document 71, 76th Congress, 1st session, 1939. *The route of the expedition through the South is described with many comparative and analytical notes. Fundamental for a study of southern Indians.*

THE FISHERMEN OF THE NORTHWEST COAST

Boas, Franz. The social organization and secret societies of the Kwakiutl Indians. USNM-AR 1895:315–738 1897.

Douglas, Frederic H. Totem poles. 7 p. DAM-L 79–80 1936. *Sums up the details of history, purpose, techniques and designs.*

Emmons, George T. The basketry of the Tlinkit. AMNH-M 3:229–277 1903. *A full description of the most typical Northwest coast basketry.*

—— The Chilkat blanket; with notes on the designs by Franz Boas. AMNH-M 3:329–400 1907. *The products of one of the four great centers of Indian weaving fully described and their designs discussed.*

Goddard, Pliny E. Indians of the Northwest Coast. 176 p. AMNH-H 10 1924. *The best popular guide to the subject.*

Gunther, Erna and Haeberlin, Herman. The Indians of Puget Sound. UW-PA 4:1–83 1930. *A good general account of the region's Indians.*

Ray, Verne F. Lower Chinook ethnographic notes. UW-PA 7:29–165 1938. *The Chinook tribe was the most important on the Columbia river in the 19th century.*

—— Cultural relations in the plateau of northwestern America. 154 p. Publications of the Frederick Webb Hodge anniversary publication fund 3. Los Angeles, Southwest Museum, 1939. *The tribes in this region link the Plains and Northwest coast areas.*

Selected Bibliography (Cont'd)

THE ESKIMO HUNTERS OF THE ARCTIC

Birket-Smith, Kaj. The Eskimos. 250 p. N. Y., Dutton, 1936. *The best general account.*

Boas, Franz. Decorative designs of Alaska needle cases. USNM-P 34:321–344 1908. *Details of designs engraved on ivory.*

Fifth Thule expedition, Reports of. Copenhagen, Gyldendalske Boghandel Nordisk Forlag, 1927. *A large number of descriptions and analyses, in English, of Eskimo culture both ancient and modern.*

Freuchen, Peter. Arctic adventure. 467 p. N. Y., Farrar & Rinehart, 1935. *Exciting stories of hardships and native life.*

Jochelson, Vladimir I. History, ethnology and anthropology of the Aleut. 91 p. CIW-P 432 1933. *A good account of the modern inhabitants of the Aleutian Islands.*

Murdock, John. Ethnological results of the Point Barrow expedition. 441 p. BAE-R 9 1892. *The Eskimo of northern Alaska described.*

Nelson, Edward W. The Eskimo about Bering Strait. 516 p. BAE-R 18 1899. *The Eskimo of western Alaska described.*

Sources of Illustrations

The following list shows the sources from which the illustrations in this book were obtained. The initials appear after the numbers of the pages on which illustrations occur. Where more than one plate appears on a page, the credit is recorded from left to right and from top to bottom..

American Museum of Natural History	AMNH
Andover Art Studios	AAS
Beckwith, Frank	B
Brooklyn Museum	BM
Cramer, Konrad	C
Denver Art Museum	DAM
Federal Arts Project, San Francisco	FASF
Fein, Philip	F
Field Museum of Natural History	FM
Gila Pueblo	GP
Golden Gate International Exposition	GGIE
Jones, Robert M.	J
Kertesz, André	K
Knee, Earnest	KE
Laboratory of Anthropology	LA
Los Angeles Museum of History, Science, and Art	LAM
Milwaukee Public Museum	MPM
Morris, Earl	M
Museum of the American Indian, Heye Foundation	MAIH
Ohio State Museum	OSM
Peabody Museum of Archaeology and Ethnology	PM
Post, Helen M.	P
Royal Ontario Museum of Archaeology	ROM
Shoeb, William	S
Steward, Julian	ST
Taylor Museum	TM
Thompson's Photography	TP
University of California	UC
University of Oklahoma	UO
University of Pennsylvania	UP
United States Bureau of Indian Affairs	USBI
United States Department of the Interior	USDI
Weston, Brett	W
Weymouth, Charles	WY

3 K	61 AMNH	93 P	125 P	153 S	181 C
11 USBI	62 AMNH	94 P	126 W	154 DAM	182 P
12 S	63 AAS	95 UP	127 S	P	183 F
S	64 MAIH	96 UP	128 BM	155 W	184 PM
13 LA USBI	65 P	97 M	129 BM	P	185 W
14 S	66 P	98 USDI	130 BM	156 W	186 PM
15 LA	67 P	99 USDI	131 P	157 P	P
17 K	68 MPM	100 DAM	132 LAM	158 C	187 MAIH
19 K	69 MPM	101 GP	DAM	159 AMNH	188 MAIH
21 K	70 OSM	102 GP	133 P	160 P	189 F
23 K	71 C	103 LAM	P	161 P	190 C
25 J	72 C	BM	134 K	162 MAIH	191 MAIH
27 WY	73 C	LAM	135 AMNH	AMNH	192 MAIH
31 K	74 P	104 TM	136 F	163 FASF	193 MAIH
33 K	75 OSM	105 PM	138 P	MAIH	194 P
35 K	76 PM	106 M	P	164 P	195 P
37 WY	77 C	107 LAM	139 P	165 C	196 MAIH
39 K	78 C	108 M	140 S	166 C	197 P
41 K	79 PM	109 PM	141 P	167 AMNH	198 K
43 WY	80 MAIH	110 PM	UP	168 C	199 USDI
45 D	81 PM	111 K	142 UP	169 C	P
47 K	82 MAIH	112 K	143 USBI	170 W	201 W
53 MAIH	83 MAIH	113 ST	144 BM	171 K	202 P
54 MAIH	84 TP	UC	P	172 C	203 USDI
55 AMNH	85 UO	114 B	145 P	173 C	204 P
56 ROM	86 BM	120 USBI	P	174 MAIH	205 P
57 UP	87 C	121 PM	146 K	175 AMNH	206 K
58 MAIH	88 C	122 S	148 W	176 S	207 K
P	89 AAS	S	149 S	177 K	208 GGIE
59 OSM	90 AAS	S	150 MAIH	178 AMNH	209 KE
60 C	91 AAS	123 W	151 P	179 P	210 K
UO	92 MAIH	124 LAM	152 FASF	180 W	K

FIFTEEN THOUSAND COPIES OF THIS BOOK HAVE BEEN PRINTED IN JANUARY 1941 FOR THE TRUSTEES OF THE MUSEUM OF MODERN ART BY THE PLANTIN PRESS, NEW YORK. THE COLOR SUPPLEMENT WAS PRINTED BY THE DUENEWALD PRINTING CORPORATION.

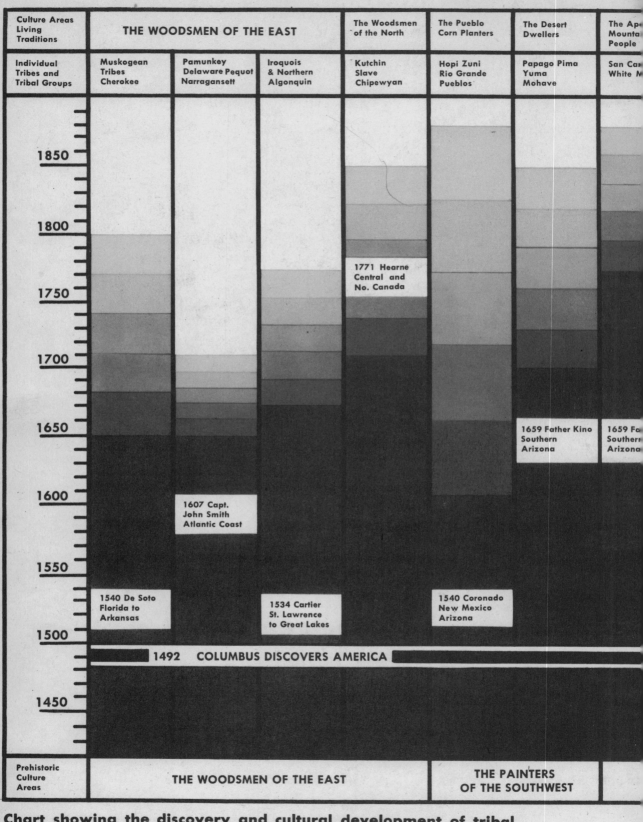

Culture Areas Living Traditions	THE WOODSMEN OF THE EAST			The Woodsmen of the North	The Pueblo Corn Planters	The Desert Dwellers	The Ape Mountain People
Individual Tribes and Tribal Groups	Muskogean Tribes Cherokee	Pamunkey Delaware Pequot Narragansett	Iroquois & Northern Algonquin	Kutchin Slave Chipewyan	Hopi Zuni Rio Grande Pueblos	Papago Pima Yuma Mohave	San Ca White M

1850

1800

1750

1771 Hearne Central and No. Canada

1700

1659 Father Kino Southern Arizona

1659 Fa Southern Arizona

1650

1607 Capt. John Smith Atlantic Coast

1600

1550

1540 De Soto Florida to Arkansas

1534 Cartier St. Lawrence to Great Lakes

1540 Coronado New Mexico Arizona

1500

1492 COLUMBUS DISCOVERS AMERICA

1450

Prehistoric Culture Areas	THE WOODSMEN OF THE EAST	THE PAINTERS OF THE SOUTHWEST

Chart showing the discovery and cultural development of tribal groups. In each column appears the name of the first historian of the regional group and the date of the exploration.